Revolution Rising

Book Two of the Tewkesbury Chronicles

by

Jo Gillespie

Revolution Rising
Book Two of the Tewkesbury Chronicles

Cover Design by Indie Designz
http://www.indiedesignz.com

Artwork by Sylvia Appleton
Proofreading and Editing by Rita M. Reali,
The Persnickety Proofreader

Revolution Rising – Jo Gillespie

S. APPLETON

Dear Reader:

The events in this novel take place in 1778, when Washington's Continental Army wintered at Valley Forge, Pennsylvania. They are true to time and place. The characters, most of whom were introduced in my first novel, *When Revolution Calls*, are fictional.

With the acceptance and success of my first novel, and encouragement from you all, I am continuing the patriotic and adventurous lives of my characters in a series I now title *The Tewkesbury Chronicles*. As I come to know and understand my characters better, I confess I enjoy them even more, and hope you will too.

Jo Gillespie

Dedicated to

My best friend for life

Linda Certo

Chapter 1

Oliver crouched in the corner of the dark, abandoned church sanctuary, his hands wracked with pain from the sub-freezing early-January temperatures. Several hours of holding his position had left his legs stiff and numb. He occasionally stood to stretch and catch glimpses of this particular Philadelphia roadway intersection buzzing with British occupation.

I'm a Tewkesbury. I can do this, he thought over and over. His father, if he were still living, would surely condemn him for his spying activities, as would the rest of his family and acquaintances back in Brookline, Massachusetts. The Tewkesburys were considered upper-class gentlemen farmers who prided themselves on noble and socially proper conduct. Spying would be viewed as conduct unbecoming.

But Oliver now knew the realities of war outweighed philosophizing about war. Since he left his home state two years earlier, these realities had altered his perspective considerably. During that time, he had seen unimaginable suffering, dismemberment and death that confirmed war truly was hell.

Oliver's hike from Valley Forge to Philadelphia had been treacherous, much more so than his fall travels from home to the winter encampment of Washington's army. He had forded the frigid Schuylkill River twice at knee depth to avoid being seen by his own troops, by loyalists heading into Philadelphia to sell their produce or by British soldiers scouting the area. Arriving in the city under cover of darkness, he found the Old Pine Presbyterian Church provided a safe, if temporary, haven and a suitable visual vantage point of the city.

He had come upon Old Pine by happenstance. As he made his way between buildings along Pine Street, he saw a church's side door agape and slipped inside. Seeing no signs the building was occupied, he decided it would be a suitable hiding place, perfectly situated in the middle of the city.

An unbearable stench of urine and feces stung Oliver's nostrils. At one end of the sanctuary, British soldiers had cut several holes in the floor to use as latrines, their excrement dropping into the basement below. At some point, the church had also been used to stable horses, their dung left behind adding to the stink. It was no wonder the building had been left vacant. Oliver considered he might have to burn the dried cakes of dung for warmth. But he dared not risk alerting the British of his location unless death by freezing was imminent.

As he surveyed the cavernous sanctuary, Oliver realized the British had desecrated the church. He assumed the missing pews had been ripped out and burned as a heat source for General Howe's fifteen thousand occupying troops, who had been quartered throughout the city and in encampments along its fringes. He explored the second-story lofts, only to find they were vacant of pews as well. After careful consideration, Oliver decided to station himself on the ground floor, in case a quick escape became necessary.

Briefly his thoughts drifted back to his stay months before in Granville, Connecticut and to the fair Rebecca White, who twice nursed him back to health—once from smallpox and once from pneumonia. Their parting words echoed through his mind.

"Promise me, Oliver, that you will take care. Promise me that you will come back to Granville, even if severely wounded like Jacob," Rebecca had pleaded, holding his hand against her cheek. Her younger brother, Jacob, had returned home missing his left arm below the elbow, a wound he suffered in the Battle of Brooklyn Heights.

"Would that I could, Rebecca. Know that my survival will be utmost on my mind," he said with a smile on his face to ease the tension of his leaving. "And know that my intent to return to you burns within me."

The memory of the last time he held her and of their last kiss, over four months ago, burned within and sustained him now.

His assignment was to make his way undetected into the belly of Philadelphia, to gather as much intelligence as possible about troop numbers, movement, condition, provisions and health. Along the way he witnessed loyalists heading into Philadelphia, their wagons loaded with poultry, root crops, cheeses and meats for sale to the British. He cursed under his breath to see such abundance when he and his comrades were half starving at Valley Forge.

As Oliver rose to take another good look through the corner of one of the eight-foot windows adorning the

3

east side of the church, he heard a slight creak of floorboard behind him. He froze. Someone else was in the building. This revelation came too late as Oliver was quickly seized from behind, a dagger held to his throat.

"Well, look what we have here," his captor breathed into his left ear. Oliver could not see who had hold of him, but his British accent immediately gave him away. "Shall I kill you now, or wait and hang you later to entertain the troops?" the man asked with a sneer. Oliver dared not grapple with his attacker, as the knife was already piercing his skin. "I think I shall do it now and be rid of you vermin on the spot," the Brit mused aloud.

"I think you shall not!" Oliver heard a loud voice exclaim from across the sanctuary.

His captor spun around in alarm and surprise, shoving Oliver out of his way to accost the intruder. The Brit stood motionless in the darkness, no doubt weighing his options, for no more than five seconds when a rifle shot plowed through him, causing him to career against the wall in the precise spot Oliver had occupied not two minutes earlier. His body slid down the wall to a sitting position, then toppled to the floor.

Astounded, Oliver shook his head in disbelief that he had come so close to being killed, then saved by… He peered into the darkness to get a glimpse of his savior as the man stepped forward, smoking musket in hand, a man he immediately recognized. "Gabriel?"

"I've no time to explain now, Oliver," Gabriel said as he lifted the fallen Oliver by the forearm. "The shot will

4

have alerted any nearby troops, who will be here in no time. It's best we move quickly."

The two men sprinted across the church sanctuary and swiftly exited through the side door into the cover of the moonless night.

Chapter 2

A year before, in June of 1776, Gabriel's mentally ill wife, Anna, took her own life in the most tragic manner. Her fragile mental state had worried Gabriel incessantly, but he never thought for an instant he would lose her. Rather, he had envisioned being her caretaker into their old age and perhaps beyond, in the afterlife.

When news of Anna's suicide spread through Granville, the townspeople were shocked and saddened. The circumstances of her death, throwing herself into an intensely hot flaming pit of wood coals during the summer-solstice gathering of local Indians, mystified not only the townspeople, but her family as well. And no one spoke of it.

After over a year, it was Gabriel's Indian farmhand, Jon Bear, who had first broached the subject of Anna's death. It had been fall harvest and all hands were laboring in the field—Gabriel's nineteen-year old daughter, Rebecca; seventeen-year old son Jacob; eleven-year old daughter, Mehti, short for Mehitable; and his sister Sarah, wife of Jon Bear. Jacob's wife, Rachael, then six months with child, kept to the kitchen to tend the fire.

Because Anna had taken her own life, Reverend Samuel Bass, Granville's former pastor who had since been run out of town in disgrace, refused her burial in the church plot. So Anna had been buried on a slight rise between two towering oaks alongside the fields, a spot on which the family focused its attention now as they briefly rested by the wagon half loaded with corn. Gabriel had been tempted on cold fall mornings to cut down those two oaks for firewood, but decided to leave them standing—a sanctuary of sorts.

"I think of Anna often when we are in this field," Jon Bear said, staring up at her isolated burial site. "I think she is content to be here." He sat cross-legged next to Mehti, his black hair drawn to a lengthy ponytail trailing down his back, his mix of colonial and Indian garb exposing his mixed allegiance.

A long silence followed. Mehti sat on the ground, her hair disheveled as usual, her lack of modesty evident as she also sat cross-legged in her smock; she bit down on an apple. As she looked up at her mother's gravestone, a lone crow alighted there momentarily; it eyed the gathering and then quickly flew off. Mehti gasped, and then locked eyes with Jon Bear as an unspoken understanding passed between them. Jon Bear held meaning in the signs of nature, as did Mehti.

"I think of her often, as well," Gabriel said, clearing his throat.

"But I still don't understand what happened," Mehti said boldly. "Why doesn't anybody ever say?"

"Mehti, please," Rebecca said in a low whisper.

"No, no—it's all right," Gabriel responded. "Mehti, I don't speak of it because, like you, I don't know what possessed your mother to…"

"She was simply so distraught for so long over the loss of her babes, I believe she could bear it no longer," Rebecca interrupted before her father could find his words. Then she added softly, "No one should feel guilt for her actions."

"Her death eats at me," Gabriel confessed to his family. "I have come to believe that my purpose on this earth lessens every day."

At this comment, Mehti jumped up and hugged her father tightly around his waist. "That's not true," she said, looking up into his eyes.

Since Anna's death, the family had noticed how Gabriel's sullen moods caused him to isolate himself more and more over time, until he barely spoke at gatherings and rarely ventured across the green to White Horse Tavern to hear news of the war. The townspeople often inquired as to his health and whereabouts. Even this brief discussion prompted by Jon Bear's comment was a rarity.

"I have been thinking for some time that I need to make amends for her loss in some way," Gabriel said. "So I've decided to join up with the Army. I served at Cambridge and joining the Army, or serving again in the militia, will perhaps put me to some good use."

"No, father!" Jacob exclaimed. "It's a different war now. You'll not only be fighting the British, but our loyalist countrymen as well. They are brazen now that the British have taken over Philadelphia and Congress has evacuated to York. Our men are setting up camp at Valley Forge, hoping on hope they will not be attacked by the British. There would be no good in your traveling there. I beg you to reconsider," he pleaded.

"You and Jon Bear can run this farm fine without me. Jacob, when I daily see the sacrifice you've already made in the war, guilt invades even more. With your mother so fragile, it wasn't possible for me to join you on Long Island; but now there is no reason for me to shirk my duty."

Gabriel White was one of the most respected and revered men in the town and surrounding farms of Granville, Connecticut. Like other local Sons of Liberty, he answered the call to Cambridge in 1775. A year later, at the age of 15, his only son, Jacob, had marched off to join Washington's forces in New York and lost his left arm at the elbow. Gabriel could stand idle no longer.

"Becca, have you heard any news from Oliver? Do you know his whereabouts?" Gabriel asked.

"I received a letter over a month ago, Father. Oliver seemed hesitant to give me his specific location, but mentioned he was on the outskirts of Philadelphia."

"I need to locate him and plan on leaving within the week."

His announcement took everyone by surprise, but the resolve in his voice kept them from questioning his decision any further.

The sun had begun to set, casting a golden glow of low fall light through the remaining cornstalks, as the family mulled over Gabriel's unexpected announcement. But the closing of the day brought closure to the conversation, and the White family silently made its way across the fields, toward the welcoming fire of their farmhouse.

Chapter 3

Oliver reasoned he and Gabriel should make their way to the outskirts of Philadelphia from the southernmost section of the city's grid of roads. Gabriel was satisfied to follow Oliver's lead, assuming him to be more knowledgeable of the city's layout. Pine Street was just a few blocks from surrounding farmland at the southern edge of town. The moonless sky allowed a perfect cover.

As they quietly crept along the cobblestone walkways, keeping close to homes and buildings, they occasionally came upon prostitutes stationed on street corners—crouched around small, impromptu fires providing minimal warmth—waiting for customers. When British General Howe entered the city months before, he immediately recognized a pressing entertainment need for his men and requisitioned 300 prostitutes from the streets of New York to buoy the men's spirits. Combining their talents with those of local prostitutes, the New York transplants found business was brisk, filling the needs of fifteen thousand troops. Luckily, no soldiers were on the streets at this hour.

Passing by a group of three ladies of the evening, the golden glow of the fire highlighting their faces, Oliver slowed his pace, unsure what kind of reception they would receive. He tipped his hat as one woman rested her gaze on his handsome face for just a moment, but said nothing as he and Gabriel continued on their way. *They are just girls*, Oliver thought. He was certain the women knew them to be patriots, but did not give them away.

"We need to get out of the city to a safe haven before daylight," Oliver told Gabriel. "I had forded Schuylkill north of here where the river runs a bit shallow. But from this far south, we'll need to cross as Gray's Ferry, which is generally guarded. It's a floating bridge. If we're detected during our crossing, we can always dive in and take the water route." Gabriel shivered at this prospect.

Within the hour, the two men came upon Gray's Ferry, which included a floating pontoon walking bridge with a rope ferry alongside, suitable for carrying up to two wagons with horses. Lamplights illuminated either side of the bridge entrance. The inky Schuylkill River was foreboding, its banks void of growth that could have otherwise provided cover. While no sentry was posted on the east side of the river, the side nearer to Oliver and Gabriel, they could see at least two sentries guarding the western egress.

Oliver crouched down on all fours and made his way to the bridge entrance; lying flat on his stomach, he proceeded to cross the bridge, inching his way across the span. Gabriel followed suit.

Once Oliver arrived within five yards of the bridge's western edge, he lay still, his eyes steadily focused on the sentries, awaiting an opportunity to right himself and bolt to the cover of a nearby stock building. Gabriel found the crossing more difficult for two reasons. First, his musket slowed him down. Second, at 45, he was slightly more than twice Oliver's age. The cold seeped into his bones like a sponge drawing water. Luckily, the sounds of the Schuylkill's ice chunks lashing against the bridge's pontoons were loud enough to camouflage their activities. Oliver strained to hear the Brits' discussions, hoping to gain any additional information that might prove useful to American forces at Valley Forge. But the sounds of the Schuylkill drowned them out as well.

Be patient, Oliver thought. *Wait for the right moment.*

Besides the posted sentries, there were no pedestrian prospects intending to cross the bridge. Oliver calculated the odds and determined they were safer waiting. But the longer they stayed prone and motionless, the colder they became as frigid river air swept like an icy shroud over their bodies. After lying perfectly still for over half an hour, Oliver noticed the two sentries turned to walk along the river bank, their backs momentarily away from the bridge opening.

"Now!" Oliver called back to Gabriel, and the two men leapt up, stiff from the cold, and hobbled silently to reach cover before the soldiers turned back again.

"We need to find shelter and soon," Gabriel said. The chill throughout his body would not be abated. From their hiding place, Oliver pointed toward a stretch of woods running along adjacent farm fields that would provide adequate concealment. The two made their way through the darkness headed west, away from Philadelphia and toward Valley Forge.

"We need to keep moving," Oliver said as the sky started to lighten in icy pastel shades of blue on the eastern horizon. "If we stop, we'll freeze to death." The men were following the Gulph Road, keeping a wary eye out for British troops on patrol. As far as they could tell, the British were keeping themselves to the comforts of Philadelphia, rarely venturing out past the Schuylkill.

"How did you ever find me?" Oliver finally asked Gabriel.

"I went first to Valley Forge and spoke with several soldiers there. It took three days before I found someone who directed me to a Captain Schmitt, who told me of your mission in the city. I concealed myself in the back of a supply wagon to enter the city and, once there, kept my search to any abandoned buildings in the hope I would find you. It seems a miracle I came upon you when I did."

Oliver patted him on the back. "There's no doubt but that I owe you my life, Gabriel.

So you've been to Valley Forge. Every manner of suffering one can imagine lies there, deaths occurring every day. At least now the cabins have been built, nearly 2,000 in all that will provide some limited shelter. But we have no stores."

A sound off in the distance caused Gabriel to signal silence, and the two men dashed, one to a sloping bank on the side of the road, the other behind the trunk of a large oak. A single horse-drawn wagon carrying two passengers came around the bend, headed in the direction of the city. The riders appeared to be farmers in Quaker garb—wide-brimmed hats on both, perhaps a father and his grown son.

As the wagon neared Gabriel and Oliver's hiding spots, Gabriel stepped out from behind the tree, musket drawn, and aimed at the older traveler. "Drop those reins and put your hands on top of your heads," he said, his head at an angle, as he glared down the barrel of his gun. Oliver scurried up the embankment and walked around to the back of the wagon. Lifting a canvas tarp, he spied a cache of produce—barrels of dried meat, packed cheeses, frozen mutton legs and small kegs of mead.

"Loyalist Quakers all too willing to aid the British and deny starving patriots a morsel to live on?" he asked sarcastically as he looked over their fine rig and strong, healthy draught horse. Oliver had seen starvation firsthand at Valley Forge and knew the flow of produce from outlying farms went not to American soldiers, but rather to the British occupying the city who were able to pay gold to keep their own troops fed. An image surfaced in his mind from his last visit to Valley Forge, an image of half-clad, emaciated men, twelve to a cabin, lying on damp straw and huddled around a fireplace at the rear, the fetid, smoky air suffocating.

"We are simply pacifists," the older man replied. "We want nothing to do with this war."

"Except to profit from it, while our men lie in squalor without a piece of bread to get them through even a day. You are traitors to the cause," Oliver bellowed at them both. "We should shoot you both here and now." The riders made no reply or attempt to explain away what was obvious to all.

"Step down, now! And keep your hands on your head!" Oliver commanded. The men descended from the wagon bench onto the road.

"Take off your coats," Gabriel said.

"But sir," the older man stammered, "We will freeze without our greatcoats." But realizing their predicament and, with little hesitation, they removed their coats and threw them on the ground. Oliver immediately grabbed them and tossed them in the back of the wagon. Then he stepped up onto the wagon bench, grabbed the reins and proceeded to turn it in a west-bound direction. Snapping the reins, the wagon began to move out as Gabriel followed, walking backward to keep his musket aimed at the loyalists.

"Please sir, I beg you, do not leave us here," the father pleaded.

"The city is six miles further. I feel certain the two of you can make it if you start running now," Gabriel said. Then he caught up with the wagon and hauled himself onto the bed as Oliver yelled a "heya" to the horse and they sped down the road, the sun rising behind them.

Oliver estimated they had another thirteen or so miles to Valley Forge, a trip that could be completed after nightfall. Now that they had a rig, hiding during daylight hours would prove a bit more difficult. The ground was frozen solid with little or no snow, but plenty of icy patches dotted the roadway. Oliver noticed a rocky outcropping ahead on the right and steered the wagon off the main road, across the field toward the rocks that would conceal the rig. The horse seemed fit enough, but would surely need sustenance at some point. He was reminded of the horses at Valley Forge that had died for lack of grain. Nearly 600 had succumbed so far this winter, their frozen carcasses piled in a heap until the spring thaw would allow them to be buried.

Their first order of business was to gather brush to light a small fire for warmth and to melt some ice for the horse and themselves. Once they completed this task, they feasted on some of the dried meat and cheese. They covered the horse with the tarp and themselves with the Quakers' greatcoats and settled in to rest throughout the day and wait for nightfall.

No sooner had they closed their eyes than they heard a rustling from a nearby tangled thicket of briars, followed by a low moan. Gabriel grabbed his musket and the two of them went to investigate. Using his musket to part the thicket, they saw before them, curled in a ball and quaking with shivers, a scantily clad black man—the blackest man either had ever seen.

"Quickly, Gabriel—we need to get him by the fire."

Gabriel and Oliver reached into the thicket and pulled the man—stiff, half frozen and unable to uncoil— from the tangled mass of briars that tore at their bare hands as well as the Negro's body. They carried him to the fire and wrapped him in one of the greatcoats.

Gabriel and Oliver exchanged a glance and, without a word spoken, read each other's mind— *runaway*.

Gabriel leaned over the man's shivering body. "What's your name, boy?" he asked.

Stuttering from the cold, the man looked up at Gabriel with his watery, wavering and bloodshot eyes and replied, "I's Hut." Then he slowly closed his eyes and drifted off to sleep.

Chapter 4

Rebecca made her way out the front door of the White farmhouse and headed for the barn in search of Jon Bear. While the winter had been particularly cold, the snow accumulation had been minimal and the pathway to the barn was icily clear. The harsh wind caused her to pull her woolen cloak tight, grasping it with both hands, as she took care with her footing. She turned her face to the wind, her cheeks stinging, to keep her loose blonde locks from obscuring her view of the pathway.

I wish Father had built the barn attached to the house, she thought, recalling the attached barns she'd seen when traveling with him in northern Massachusetts to visit his aunts and uncles. She envied Jon Bear's easy access to the livestock. When Jon Bear and her Aunt Sarah were wed the summer before, Jon Bear and her father, Gabriel, built a lean-to addition to the barn to provide them their own living quarters. A simple opening had been cut in the wall between their quarters and the barn, and a door affixed with leather straps so they could pass easily between the barn and their one room.

Rebecca was certain Jon Bear would be milking their two cows at this early hour. It had been Jacob's chore, but milking with one hand had frustrated Jacob, who eventually abandoned the task. *Jacob's limitations could hamper my plans,* she thought momentarily.

Rebecca decided to visit Sarah first, rather than go directly to speak with Jon Bear. Sarah answered the door wrapped in her shawl, a poker in her hand. The previous fall, Jon Bear had built his new bride not only a bed frame, which now sat in the corner of the room laden with straw, but a huge stone fireplace that provided heat for warmth and cooking. Although their lean-to was small, Sarah had made it cozy with window curtains sewn from her calico wedding dress. She hoped one day to own a rug. Other wedding gifts included a table and two chairs that occupied the center of the room, and a lone chair by the hearth, a gift from Gabriel.

"Good morning, Aunt Sarah. I need to speak with Jon Bear. Is he tending the cows?" Rebecca asked as she lowered the hood of her cloak and rubbed the chill from her hands, taking in the warmth of the fireplace.

"He should be in shortly," Sarah replied. She stood next to Rebecca, stoking the fire, the flames' glow highlighting the huge wine-stain birthmark that cascaded down the side of her face. The vision reminded Rebecca of the hardship and persecution her aunt had faced throughout her life until coming to Granville. She was now accepted by not only the townsfolk, but also Jon Bear's tribe, who revered her, the birthmark viewed as a sign she was chosen by the Great Spirit. Since Gabriel left to join Oliver in Pennsylvania two weeks prior, Jon Bear and Sarah both helped considerably with the farm.

Rebecca began pacing the floor, mulling over the proposition she wanted to discuss with Jon Bear.

"And how is baby Anna?" Sarah asked.

"She is growing stronger every day. And Rachael has taken to motherhood with such tenderness. I am certain she is quite exhausted, but her attachment to the baby brings out her maternal instincts, so she does not succumb to her tiredness. I quite admire her. How proud I would be if I were to become, one day, half the mother she has been to Anna."

Sarah saw Rebecca's want and, stroking her back, replied, "You will be a mother one day, Rebecca. I am sure of it."

"And if you are my midwife as you were for Rachael, I'm sure all will be well."

The two of them were gazing at the fire in silence when Jon Bear swung open the door to the barn and entered, a pail of milk held at his side. He tipped his hat to Rebecca and handed the pail to Sarah. Rebecca searched his face to read his mood, but only noted tiredness around his eyes. She wasn't certain of his age and never asked about it, but guessed him to be in his late 40s, not much older than her aunt.

Rebecca knew Jon Bear to be a man of few words and decided to make her full plea to him in earnest, and then wait for his response. The two women seated themselves at the table as Jon Bear reached for his pipe, packed it with tobacco and, using a pair of fire tongs, lit the pipe with a burning ember. He sat back in his chair, certain Rebecca had something on her mind.

"Jon Bear, I am here to request your assistance," Rebecca began. Taking a deep breath, she began her plea. "Oliver has been at Valley Forge since December, and Father has been gone now for two weeks and no doubt has arrived there as well. We hear news of the horrid conditions there with requests for food, clothing and assistance. I am beginning to feel much like Father did before he left—that I am of little use sitting here in Granville, ruminating on the difficulties our troops face."

She paused, waiting for some acknowledgement from Jon Bear's stone face. His eyes remained locked on the flames, squinting as pipe smoke drifted toward the ceiling. She took another breath and proceeded.

"I wish you to accompany me to Valley Forge."

Jon Bear's face remained expressionless.

"I can be of tremendous help to our troops there. We can bring supplies—food, quilts, clothing collected from the townsfolk. I can cook, sew and tend to the sick. You need not stay—just transport me there."

Jon Bear continued his gaze into the fire.

"Jacob and Sarah can manage the farm," she added. His lack of response rattled her a bit; she stood and began pacing back and forth in front of the fire. "I'm sure you think me frivolous, or unaware of the dangers involved in such a trip. But like my father, I feel I must do this. I am stronger than you may realize."

"Why didn't you leave with your father?"

"I was hesitant. I thought about asking him, but I lost my courage and I have regretted it ever since," she replied.

"It's February."

"Yes, of course, I know it is February," Rebecca replied in frustration, "but I have savings to cover our lodging. The trip is between two hundred and three hundred miles, I believe. Please, Jon Bear. I cannot do this alone and I cannot sit here waiting for word as I did when

Jacob, Jessie and Oliver went to join Washington in 'seventy-six. That was emotional torture for all of us. I feel that same dread welling up in me now. You know the ways of survival during this time of year, Jon Bear, and I would feel quite secure having you as my escort."

"The roads are bad," Jon Bear said, knocking the ashes from his pipe onto the hearth.

"Yes, I know the roads are bad, but many of the rivers are frozen and easier to cross. We can take the wagon and the two mules that now stand in the barn, day upon day, not the least bit useful this time of year."

Again Jon Bear's silence left Rebecca anxious, but she held her counsel, allowing him time to ponder her request.

Seconds later, the outside door swung open and Mehti bounded in. Twirling around, she pushed the door shut with her back, straining against the wind. Mehitable Mercy White spent many of her winter days in the company of Sarah and Jon Bear. A precocious tomboy eager to learn all she could from Jon Bear, Mehti would also keep company with Sarah, helping her churn butter or spin wool. Today she came to help make cheese.

Mehti removed her mittens and glanced around the room; she immediately realized she had interrupted a serious adult conversation.

"What are you doing here, Mehti?" Rebecca asked, slightly annoyed at the interruption.

"Um... I came to help Aunt Sarah make the cheese?" Mehti replied, phrasing her statement as a question as her eyes shifted from face to face. "What's going on?'

Rebecca shook her head in exasperation. "Well you might as well know. Jon Bear and I are embarking on a trip to Valley Forge."

"We are discussing a trip to Valley Forge," Jon Bear corrected.

"Oh goody!" Mehti screeched, clapping her hands together. "How exciting—when are we leaving?"

"Not you, Mehti. You'll be needed here. The trip will be taken by Jon Bear and me," Rebecca said.

"May be taken," Jon Bear said, his voice flat.

"But I could go, too," Mehti pleaded. "I can do almost everything you can do," she argued to her sister. "Plus I know how to shoot a bow and arrow… right, Jon Bear?"

Jon Bear repacked and relit his pipe.

"Don't be ridiculous, Mehti. It will be difficult enough for Jon Bear and me to make the trip. You need to stay here and we will discuss this no further," Rebecca said.

Mehti folded her arms across her chest and stomped her foot to the floor, a dour expression on her face.

"You're a child!" Rebecca exclaimed. "You'll keep to the house."

Mehti wheeled around, swung open the door and exited in a huff of protest, yanking the door shut behind her.

After a few moments, Jon Bear said, "There would be the British to contend with."

"We'll skirt the cities they've laid claim to. I understand they hunker down well and luxuriate in their winter quarters of Newport, New York and Philadelphia—fat and happy. From what we've heard, they barely bother to patrol in winter months," Rebecca said, feeling a bit hopeful.

Looking directly at Rebecca, Jon Bear replied, "I will think on this matter."

Chapter 5

The hull of the 65-foot sloop, *Josephine,* languished at the end of a New London wharf, the frigid crystalline Thames River lapping at her sides, ropes straining and creaking in the wind. On this brightest of winter days, below deck the hold's cavity was dark and dank, like walking into a damp cave. Smells of vinegar and fish permeated the air.

As Rebecca and Jon Bear made their way backward down the sea ladder, minimal daylight from the aft hatch highlighted a store of boxes, barrels and sacks toward the center of the hold. Beyond that, within the belly of the boat, stood a small cast-iron stove elevated on bricks and encased in sand, the only heat source aboard. In the vessel's aft, Rebecca saw several hammocks strung between beams, their home for the next week or more. In both the bow and stern of the boat, round ample metal chamber pots sat in wait and full view against the hull, bound securely on their outer sides by planking to keep them stationary in the roughest of seas.

The decision to travel by water was not Rebecca's, as she was terrified of the water. But she had to content herself with Jon Bear's willingness to escort her, no matter the way. It took almost a week of persuasion and pleading, not only to Jon Bear, but also Jacob, to gain their support for her earnest and risky plan to travel to Valley Forge.

"I stand here asking what Father would do," Jacob said to his sister the first time she shared her scheme with him. "I dare say he would disapprove of anything that would put you in harm's way. Granted, there are those women who travel with and support the troops as you intend, but it's no life for you Rebecca. I don't think you realize how hostile it will be."

"I have been close to the war and lost my family to it," his wife Rachael chimed into the discussion as she laid her needlework in her lap. "I would certainly never think of entertaining such a notion myself at this time in my life with little Anna dependent upon me; but I think Rebecca is being courageous to venture forth, and I give her credit for her desire to help the cause in any way possible."

Mehti sat, as usual immodestly cross-legged on the floor, pouting as they all gathered in the sitting room by the fire, Jacob taking charge of his father's wingback chair in his absence. It angered her that the family did not take seriously her request to also join the war effort. Most folks in her family and in Granville saw her as a scrappy and hardy young girl, weaned on the ways of the woods with Jon Bear's help. Surely she would have much to contribute.

"You're too young, Mehti. I realize you are strong and capable, but I would be fearful it would endanger you. It is enough that I put myself at risk, I need not risk your life as well," Rebecca said.

Her determination taking hold, Mehti continued her argument. "I've heard that babes are born among the troop followers and they carry on with children in tow. So if babes can be at the encampments, why can't I?" she reasoned.

"Enough!" Jacob said. "Mehti, you're to stay here. Besides Rachael and I need your help with the baby."

"And I need your help with the chores," her Aunt Sarah added.

Mehti ran up to her room, angry and disappointed. Rebecca made a mental note to reprimand her for such a display.

"She will calm down in due time," Jacob said.

"I agree to be your escort, Rebecca, but we would travel better by boat than by land this time of year. And, barring adverse weather, it will be quicker. The British will be patrolling the waters, but if we travel by a smaller, unarmed vessel, they are unlikely to give attention," Jon Bear said.

"But that won't allow us to haul goods. All we would be able to take is what we can carry on our backs," Rebecca said. "I had hoped we'd be able to provide food and goods to our men."

"There are too many difficulties traveling by wagon. I would never attempt it. Traveling by boat is our only hope," Jon Bear replied. Jacob nodded in agreement, having traveled by wagon from Fishkill, New York to Granville in the spring of '77, an arduous, difficult journey.

"Very well—ship's passage rather than inn lodging," Rebecca acquiesced. "My purse will allow for that."

Everyone looked to one another now that the decision had been made, and reflected in silence on the risks of the proposed venture.

Two days later, Jon Bear brought the wagon around to the front of the White farmhouse, the home's dark-red shingles glistening from the misting rain of a brief warm spell.

The warmer weather might present melting problems on the roadway, Jacob thought. A frozen surface often meant easier travel and lesser likelihood a wheel would find a deep rut.

Jon Bear had harnessed both mules for their twelve-mile ride to New London. Sarah had agreed to go with them, and then drive the team back. At the time of their leaving, Mehti was nowhere in sight, which was disappointing to Sarah who hoped Mehti would come along for the ride, keeping her company on the return trip.

"She's run off brooding, I am sure," Jacob said as he came to bid his sister and Jon Bear farewell. "I saw her run out to the barn not too long ago, taking solace with the cows, no doubt."

"Please do give her my love, Jacob. She will get over this, I am sure," Rebecca said.

They had gathered and bundled up as many supplies as they each felt reasonably able to carry and, storing them under a tarp, climbed atop the wagon seat, three abreast, as Jon Bear took the reins and led the team onto the roadway. Halfway through their trip, the rain had let up, the sun partially drying the women's woolen hooded cloaks.

Unlike Newport and New York, which were held by the British, the coastal towns of Connecticut were patriot territory—New London a strong Whig town. Arrival at the wharf had been chaotic with dock workers and passengers weaving their way to and from various boats moored alongside. As they exited the wagon, Sarah and Jon Bear embraced in farewell, and Rebecca hugged her aunt as well.

"Take care, both of you, and return safe and sound," Sarah said. "I will miss you both so."

The two anxious travelers turned and headed down the wharf to locate their boat. Rebecca had only been to the city's waterfront once before and had not remembered it being so busy and congested. It was a bit of a trial to find the *Josephine* among the myriad bobbing boats. Now that they were below deck, Rebecca and Jon Bear chose adjacent hammocks and dropped their parcels beneath to claim their sleeping space. There seemed to be no other passengers on board. Toward the bow of the ship on the other side of the stowage, through dim bow hatchway light, Rebecca saw additional hammocks she assumed were used by deck hands.

No sooner had Rebecca righted herself in a sitting position in her hammock with some difficulty, than the ship's young captain came bounding down the ladder with the agility of a monkey.

"Ah, I see you are settling in," he said to Rebecca and Jon Bear, and introduced himself as Captain Treadwell, a name Rebecca though humorous for a ship's captain.

"I heard we had a young woman on board, and I wanted to welcome you personally," he said to Rebecca.

"And is this your manservant?" he asked, glancing at Jon Bear who was dressed in his usual breeches, tunic, vest and greatcoat; his jet-black Algonquin hair, tied into a ponytail, hung down his back.

"This is Jon Bear, my escort and our employed farm hand," Rebecca replied to distinguish him from an indentured servant or slave. "We seek to join my father at Valley Forge to help with the war effort."

The Captain smiled at them smugly as if to say, *you are likely both fools without knowing.* He kept his counsel, however, not wanting to offend so comely a young woman. Clearing his throat, he immediately changed his demeanor to provide them instructions. "As you can see, you are the only travelers on this boat. All others are crew. We rarely have travelers this time of year. We leave within the hour, or as soon as my men are finished loading our cargo. We head for Wilmington, with an expected travel time of between eight to twenty-two days, depending on the weather. You are to stay below deck unless you have my verbal permission to go above, which I will allow as often as conditions permit. The fresh air is renewing on a voyage such as this. We can provide a basin of heated water once daily for cleansing. Food will be limited to dried fish and cheese, perhaps once a day. We have some stored apples as well—maybe even some dried prunes. In the event of rough seas, you may be lashed to the hull for your own protection. If my men disturb you in any way, please notify me immediately. Do you have any questions?"

"None at this time," Rebecca replied.

"Very well," the Captain said. "Then we shall hope for calm seas and pleasant travel." He turned abruptly and scaled the sea ladder as quickly as he descended.

Mehti crouched between two sacks of corn meal, out of sight but within hearing distance, taking in the Captain's every word. She marveled at how easy it had been to slip into and out of the wagon bed, unnoticed, the most difficult and anxious part of her journey being access to the hold. With so many crewmembers on deck entering and exiting the hold, she had to wait for the right moment to rise up from her hiding place behind the mast and slip down the sea ladder.

Now she sat in her concealed location, waiting for the boat to depart, so there could be no question that she would be on her way to Valley Forge, as well.

Chapter 6

Oliver woke to a deep chill that invaded his body as if a permanent resident. He was sure lying still through the night, even with the greatcoat atop his own, brought him close to a frozen death.

What he was not sure of was whether their newfound traveler would still be at their campsite come morning. Peering over the collar of his coat, he noticed Gabriel's back turned away from him, his body motionless.

"Gabriel!" Oliver shouted, to no response. "Gabriel!" he shouted again. Only the Negro, Hut, stirred from his sleep. Oliver crawled over to Gabriel's side, shaking him. "Gabriel, Gabriel, wake up." A lightning bolt of fear jolted his senses. Could Gabriel have succumbed to the frigid night air?

Hut was now wide awake and taking in the rush of activity as Oliver called out Gabriel's name, slapping his face repeatedly. Moments passed before Gabriel responded with a low, weak moan. Oliver reached under Gabriel's coat and began rubbing his arms frantically, in an attempt to warm him. He turned to Hut. "Can you make a fire?"

"Yessa," Hut replied and scurried off to gather tall dried grasses and twigs in the nearby woods. Within a few minutes Hut returned and Oliver handed him his flints. It took no time for Hut to start a small fire. Oliver laid his body down next to Gabriel's, still rubbing the warmth back into him. Hut repeated his foray into the woods in search of additional wood, returning with an armload to keep the fire going.

"Hut, will you help me warm him?" Oliver asked.

"Yessa," Hut said, looking at Oliver inquisitively, uncertain exactly how he could help.

"Lie down nestled at his back and I will do the same at his front."

Hut did as he was told, and the two men sandwiched Gabriel between them, a half-moon of bodies hoping to ward off the chill that could so easily have taken them all. They lay there over half an hour, the mass of their bodies, along with the adjacent fire, gradually warming them enough to ensure the worst had passed. Gabriel was finally roused and seemed lucid.

"Quickly, Gabriel," Oliver pleaded. "We must get you moving." Oliver and Hut grabbed beneath Gabriel's arms and began to walk him around the campfire, circling repeatedly so his body would begin generating its own heat.

Gabriel finally began talking. "I think I can walk on my own," he said, and the two men let go of him as he continued to circle the fire, which had taken hold and was now generating considerable heat. Oliver went to the wagon, returning with some rations of food, as the three men settled themselves around the fire to share cheese and dried sausage.

Hut ate as though he hadn't eaten in days, although he had consumed a meal just the night before. Oliver believed his appetite must be from the uncertainty of his next meal. Glancing over at him as they sat in front of the fire, Oliver again noted the blackness of his skin. He guessed Hut's age at perhaps 25. He was of medium build and appeared to be strong and healthy, with broad shoulders. His dark, nappy hair was matted and askew, and his large, black eyes were like cannon balls, piercing and intelligent and void of whites. His nose was broad and flared at the nostrils, as expected of his kind. But his lips were not as full as one would expect.

He turned to Hut. "I'm Oliver and this is Gabriel. Hut, that's an unusual name."

Yessa," Hut replied.

"How did you come by such a name?"

"De mule, she die," Hut replied.

Gabriel and Oliver shared a glance. Finally Gabriel said, "And…"

"An so de massa, he put me to dat plow. He say, "Hut, hut" an den he crack dat whip. Dem niggas what on da farm, dey call me Hut afta dat."

"How old were you when your master hooked you to the plow?" Oliver asked solemnly.

Hut put down his cheese, swallowed hard and scratched his head in thought. "I's maybe ten? Dat be my job evry spring to plant da tobacco and evry fall too. I's a strong nigga. I's like my mammy. She a strong breeder—fifteen chillun," he bragged.

"Where are you from, Hut? Are you a free man? Do you have your papers?" Gabriel asked in a flurry of questions.

"I's from Richmon'. Don't got no papers—jus a note from my missus. She tell me to git, quick like, so I git.

She say go nort, so I go nort to dat place she call Albany cus she got family der."

Hut could see by the looks on the faces of Oliver and Gabriel they wanted to hear more of his story. He wasn't sure if he should tell it, but he knew he needed help, and these two men seemed taken to him and his plight. And so, on that freezing February morning as the three men sat around their campfire, Hut told them how he came to be free, yet hiding in a thicket in the woods of Pennsylvania.

Hut's mother came originally from New Orleans as a young slave woman, sold on the block to a speculator who drove her and several other slaves by wagon to Georgia, where slave labor was in high demand. Rose Jumbai was her name. She was sold again on the auction block in Savannah to a family who needed a housemaid who could also work the plantation fields.

"My mammy say dey bid $500 for her cus she young and strong—cud breed babes to make da massa a rich slave owner. She say dey strip her on dat block and the overseer, he see she got no marks, an dat be good."

Hut was born on the farm in Georgia, along with several of his brothers and sisters, who were all as black as he, since the slave the master chose for Rose to breed with was black as coal. Their master treated them well, as long as they worked the farm and Rose continued to propagate and bring him wealth. They'd take her babies away at one year of age, so Rose would stop nursing and be able to bear another child. Lactating women rarely got pregnant.

"Some of dem babies stay. Some be sold at five. I's got to stay wit my mammy."

After over six years in Savannah, Hut's owner died of typhoid fever and his slaves were sold off to pay his debts. Another speculator purchased Hut, his mother and three of her other children. But his father was sold to a local plantation owner, which was the last Hut saw of his father.

The speculator took them to Richmond, Virginia, where they were sold at auction to a tobacco farmer.

"I 'member mammy crying to keep us wit her, and de new massa, man name Jenkins, he say no. But de missus be der too, and she say, 'Bring dem chillun,' an so we all go."

Hut's new master was the owner who had hooked him to the plow—a mean and hard-drinking man whose slaves steered clear of him whenever he was on the bottle. But the person his master treated with unbridled cruelty was not a slave, but his wife, Hannah. When her husband went on a drunken rant, Hannah would often seek shelter among the slaves in their quarters, her bruised and battered face a testimony to his cruelty. Such was the case on Hut's last night in Richmond. The slaves who sheltered her once again could hear Jenkins screaming her name like a crazed man as he searched their plantation home and surrounding grounds.

"Den dis time he com' into our cabin. De missus, she hid behine us under de table. Massa see her and drag her by de hair. We stay back cus he got de pistol and cus he da massa."

Throughout that night, the slaves heard the sounds of Jenkins beating his wife, swearing at her, and her wailing. Hut would never forget her wailing. Then from their cabin, Hut and the other slaves heard a gun fire, and rushed into the house to see if their mistress was injured or killed.

The master lay still in a pool of blood on the bedroom floor, his wife standing over his body, his pistol held limply in her hand. Her face was bloodied as well from his battering, and her clothes were torn, exposing her breasts, which were covered with welts. She was trembling, unable to speak and seemed to be in a trance.

"My mammy, she tend to da missus—cover her up, sat her down. She say we got ta clean up dat mess to help da missus."

Hut and two other slaves wrapped Jenkins' body in a quilt and carried it out to the grounds, where they quickly dug a grave and buried him. Rose cleaned up Mistress Jenkins, gave her a shot of whiskey and put her to bed. The next day, with dazed eyes that stared blankly, Mistress Jenkins came out to the slave cabins and told her eight slaves they could leave—that she was freeing them. Rose said she would not leave Mistress Jenkins, but advised Hut, her eldest, to head north to freedom. Mistress Jenkins told Hut to seek out her family in Albany and wrote a letter that Hut handed to Oliver.

"Do you know what became of your mistress?" Gabriel asked.

"No sa. I don know iffin she turn hersef in or not. But my mammy, she won't leave da missus side. So she stay wit da kids. Da odder slaves, they scatter like mice and leave dat place. I get dis far."

Oliver glanced down at a brief note written with a shaky hand. He read it out loud.

> *Dearest Mother and Father-*
> *This is my slave, Hut, who I grant his freedom and who*
> *I ask that you take in as a hired servant if at all possible.*
> *Your Loving Daughter,*
> *Hannah*

The three men sat in silence for a while. Oliver Tewkesbury's family was known throughout his home township of Brookline, Massachusetts, and indeed throughout the County of Norfolk, as staunchly opposed to slavery. His mind conjured up a recollection—the image of his father, Ezra, as First Selectman of Brookline, at the head of the town tavern table, surrounded by town leaders, delivering his impassioned plea for support of modification of the Massachusetts Constitution to outlaw slavery. He had always been so proud of the stands his father took, and believed, as his father did, in the worth and dignity of every man. As far as Oliver knew, that law was yet to be put in place. But Oliver's family had never owned a slave and never would. Gabriel knew of no slaves in Granville, but had heard rumors of their harsh treatment, and now knew an instance where it proved true.

Gabriel spoke first. "Hut, you are a free man and therefore free to do as you wish. But it is very unlikely you'll make it to Albany alive this time of the year, unless you have help along the way. We are on our way to Valley Forge and cannot assist you in your journey."

"Perhaps he could come to Valley Forge with us," Oliver suggested.

"Don't be foolish," Gabriel replied. "The man has no papers."

"I could claim he came from Massachusetts with me and vouch that he is a free man."

"At what risk? I think this unwise," Gabriel argued.

"None that I can think of," Oliver said after a few moments of contemplation. Turning to Hut, he put the question to him. "Hut, what do you think about joining the Patriots who wage war against the British?"

"I donno."

"Have you ever shot a rifle?" Gabriel asked.

"Humph. Ain't no whitey ever gib dis nigga a gun," Hut said with a smile on his face.

"I could train you," Oliver said.

"Oliver, for God's sake, think what you're saying, man," Gabriel continued.

"Dey got food at dis Valley Forge?" Hut asked. "If dey gots food, I can fight."

"Then it's done," Oliver said, ignoring Gabriel's pleas.

The moon rose up as the fire burned down; the men tended to the horse, then began packing for the night time drive to Valley Forge.

Chapter 7

The apparition took shape before Rebecca in the morning hours of their first day at sea. Captain Treadwell had charted a course around the eastern end of Long Island, sailing west southwest along the southern shore, headed for the New Jersey coast. His experience taught him to avoid Long Island Sound and the waters surrounding New York Harbor, so rife with British vessels. If he kept to his course, his small, unarmed boat would most likely go unnoticed. He even intended to travel by night, when the moon was right and he could get his bearing by the stars.

The air below deck was suffocating as if Rebecca's head laid below a down pillow, and she was determined to go above as often as possible, even in the frigid ocean air. The day was cold, but the skies were clear as the *Josephine's* prow sliced through the murky, unforgiving Atlantic. On the morning they disembarked, Rebecca had stood near the bow, wrapped in her cloak, holding her hood tight to her face. The moist salt spray whipped at her, blurring her vision. What discomfort she experienced only made her feel more alive. She had heard about seasickness, but had not been bothered by it in the least. The roll and pitch of the boat just lulled and soothed. Jon Bear was not so fortunate and spent much of his time at the railings.

But just knowing they were well underway and headed to Wilmington, only 32 miles from Valley Forge, filled Rebecca with an exhilaration she did not anticipate.

Better than sitting home, a lady in waiting, she thought. From this vantage point, she could see Jon Bear holding tight to the lines, looking off the stern at a shrinking Long Island. He too seemed more at home closer to the elements, even though it caused his illness. She noted Captain Treadwell keeping an eye on her, and she appreciated his unwavering concern for her safety.

Turning away from the wind, she headed for the forward hatch, spinning in place to ease her way backward down the ship's ladder. As she reached the bottom, turned and lowered her hood, the apparition appeared in the form of her sister, Mehti, standing perfectly still a few feet in front of the wood stove, hands closed in front of her. A glow from the stove's embers set off her ethereal silhouette. Of course Rebecca missed her family and worried for her sister, but why would Mehti's spirit come to her now she wondered. She had always hoped to see a vision of her deceased mother, but alas, it never happened, although she dreamed of her frequently.

And then it spoke to her.

"Becca, I'm so sorry. Please don't be angry with me."

Rebecca shook her head, thinking perhaps she was having a hallucination. But Mehti stepped toward her.

"I could not just sit idle and not be with you, Jon Bear, father and Oliver. Please forgive me. I will not be a burden, I promise."

Rebecca's mind quickly shifted to reality.

"Mehitable Mercy White—what have you done?" Rebecca bellowed. A rush of anger swept over her. "You reckless child! You very reckless child!" she scolded.

From topside, Jon Bear heard the commotion and began his descent into the hold. He was shocked to see Mehti standing in the middle of the boat, a look of contrition on her face. Walking over to her, Jon Bear put his hand on her shoulder and said, "You have made a grave mistake, Mehti, one that may cost you your life."

"A stowaway!" Rebecca bellowed. "What are we to tell the captain? And how much will this cost us? Our funds are limited."

"I could stay hidden for the rest of the voyage," Mehti suggested.

"Don't be foolish," Rebecca replied, pacing back and forth now. "We must let him know at once that you are on board."

Moments later Captain Treadwell joined their little gathering. "What have we here?" he asked. "A stowaway?"

Rebecca flushed with embarrassment. "Captain Treadwell, I do apologize for this breach by my sister, Mehti. She is a pigheaded child who has not kept to her place. Of course we will pay her passage as well, and I promise you, she will not interfere in any way," she declared, her eyes fixed on Mehti, whose head now hung low. "She can share a hammock with me, Captain, and Jon Bear and I will keep her close."

"No need, Miss White. There is an extra hammock to the stern of the ship that will accommodate her," Treadwell replied.

"But sir…" Rebecca said.

"It's decided, and I'll hear no more of it," he said curtly. And then he briskly made his way up the ladder.

The next two days aboard the *Josephine* went without incident, the weather faring in their favor. It was not unusual for a hearty storm to kick up the seas this time of year, but they had the good fortune to be traveling during a relative warm spell with moderate seas. Mehti kept out of sight as much as possible and rarely ventured topside. They dined on salt cod, oatmeal and cheese, which sufficed.

On the third night of their voyage, Rebecca was woken first by the aroma of alcohol stinging her nostrils, then by the alarm of a hand thrust over her mouth. She could barely make out her attacker in the absolute darkness of the hold. He whispered in her ear in his drunken slur, "A lovely package we have here—one for the taking, I daresay." His free hand traveled up and down her torso, groping and kneading, and then he reached for her skirts. Rifling them up, his hand delved higher and higher as she struggled to release herself from his grip.

"Keep still, wench," he warned as he bore his hand down harder on her mouth. "I should hate to let all know you've teased me to this point—coming on deck every day, swaying your hips about."

In a panic, Rebecca tried to shift her gaze from side to side. Where was Jon Bear? His hammock was in the bay next to hers. Was he topside again, taken with seasickness? She tried to scream, but only a mumble of sound made its way from her throat. She could scarcely believe this would be her fate. It was always Oliver she dreamed would take her in a loving caress. This vile person was violating her on every front. She thought she might throw up and tried to hold back from retching.

He noted her calmer demeanor. "Yes, that's right, missy. Nobody's gonna hear you," he said as he proceeded to pull down the knickers beneath her skirts. "Your Indian friend isn't here to save you," he jeered. She felt his grubby hand pawing at her stomach and she was overcome by panic, squirming as violently as she could, grabbing at his probing arm to stop his assault.

"Arghhh!" he yelled out as he released Rebecca suddenly and fell to the floor. Behind him, in the dim light from the hatchway, stood Mehti, a cast-iron frying pan in her hands that she had slammed into his back like the swing of an ax. He fell on all fours and attempted to right himself when Mehti struck him again, on the head this time, with all the force the determined eleven-year-old could muster. Jon Bear came running down, a lantern in his hand. Sprawled on the boat's floor was Captain Treadwell, knocked unconscious.

Rebecca who had lowered her skirts, looked ashamedly at Jon Bear and burst into tears.

"I should have been here to protect you, Rebecca. This will never happen again," Jon Bear said as Rebecca slid off her hammock, still trembling as he held her close.

The commotion led crew members to gather around. Staring down at their captain, one of them finally spoke up.

"Don't take no never mind, miss. The Captain gets ideas in his head from the drink. But we'll get him to his cabin, miss. Don't take no never mind, is all." And they swiftly lifted the Captain and carried him off to his room.

Then, turning from Jon Bear, Rebecca knelt before Mehti, taking her into her arms. The exasperating child had saved her virtue, maybe even her life. "Thank you Mehti," she said, wiping away the tears that were streaming down her face.

"I told you I would be a help," Mehti replied matter of factly.

"Yes. Yes, you did, Mehti," Rebecca replied. "Perhaps I should listen to you more often." Rebecca took a deep breath, followed by a jagged exhale, still trembling.

For the rest of their voyage, Jon Bear never let Rebecca or Mehti out of his sight, and Captain Treadwell kept his distance from all three of his passengers, spending most of his time in his cabin, his first mate manning the wheel. No mention was ever made of Mehti's passage fee.

When they finally reached Wilmington, gathered up their things and headed for the gangplank, the Captain was nowhere in sight. But what were in sight were sharply dressed British soldiers patrolling up and down the wharf, the first British soldiers any of them had ever seen. Undaunted, Rebecca strode directly up to one of them.

"Sir, please excuse me, but can you point us to suitable lodging?"

"Well, miss, there's the Brandywine Village Inn," he said in a thick cockney accent as he scanned up and down their common travel attire. "It's a few blocks from here and across the Christina River Bridge. Just beyond there is Buck's Tavern. It's a bit rowdy, sailors with their grog and such."

"Thank you so much. You have been most kind."

The three travelers turned and began their walk through inches of new-fallen snow.

Chapter 8

Oliver, Gabriel and Hut entered Valley Forge in the middle of a heavy mid-February snow, the three men sitting abreast on the wagon seat as if equals. The winter thus far had seen little snow, but severe cold, followed by temperate weather, then a refreeze that left the ground as rough as a flat of nails. Given that a third of the 12,000 men at the encampment were shoeless, walking on the rough frozen ground left their feet bleeding and swollen. For those who had shoes, the frozen ground chewed up their leather soles. Ironically, the new soft snow would provide relative comfort to bare feet, and spare leather soles.

Several men, those with watch coats, guarded the camp entrance and waved the men on to the large expanse of plateau known as Valley Forge. The area was surrounded by partially felled timber used to build huts, along with steep-sided and denuded hills known as Mount Joy and Mount Misery to the west, and the Schuylkill River to the north, all providing strategic safety from a possible British attack.

Hut sat wide-eyed, taking in the spectacle before him, his expression conveying his good fortune to never have gone without food or clothing. He wondered if perhaps he had made a mistake in coming here. In spite of the inclement weather, the camp was a bustle of activity. A few men milled back and forth across a grand parade, some shoeless, others shirtless, many in full dress. Oliver caught Hut's expression and tried to explain their situation.

"These men have been without proper food and clothing since arriving here in December. We have men scouring the countryside for food from locals on a promise to pay; but with the British paying with gold coin, only the most dedicated patriots oblige us. Presently, this many men are capable of consuming nearly thirty-five-thousand pounds of meat a day, and their appetites for bread are just as huge."

"So der's no food here?" Hut asked.

"There will be, as soon as Congress allocates funds," Gabriel replied. "At first the men were not allowed to leave the camp for fear they'd harass the local farmers. But now they're being allowed to leave to hunt raccoon, opossum, skunk, squirrel… and that's how some get by."

Looking around the huge encampment, Hut soaked in the vision of what looked like two thousand wooden cabins hewn from logs, all about the same size. Some were partially buried underground, their rise just four feet above ground level. Every cabin had exiting its roof a stream of smoke from fires that provided the heat source that kept shirtless and blanket-less men as warm as possible in this deep mid-winter freeze.

"Each cabin holds twelve men," Oliver explained. "The officers' huts are to the right over there. They're a bit bigger and hold maybe six to eight officers. To the rear of the cabins are tents. Those are for wives and children of military, and for service women following the troops."

As they passed by one of the enlisted men's cabins, a shirtless, barefoot soldier stepped outside the cabin to relieve himself, and then quickly turned to resettle himself by the warmth of the fire.

"To the latrine ditch with you!" Oliver yelled at the soldier. But it was too late. The deed had already been done. Given their lack of clothing, the men were understandably reluctant to walk the distance to a designated latrine ditch. But sanitation issues, particularly for those men who refused to even leave their huts to relieve themselves, were root causes of illness at the camp.

On the far side of the open field, Hut saw a huge wooden structure, maybe eighty feet long.

"What dey keep in der?" he asked.

"That's a general-assembly building. Men congregate there for meetings, and we distribute goods and food from that location," Oliver explained as the wagon slowly made its way along the south side of the camp.

Up ahead a skeletal, ragtag mob of soldiers was approaching, guns and fists raised in the air, as they shouted, "No meat! No meat!" in protest of their lack of provisions going on two days.

Officers ran alongside them, swords drawn, shouting at the mob to cease and desist and return to their cabins immediately. But the men were only silenced momentarily when they spied the loaded wagon heading toward them.

"Food!" one of the men yelled, and the entire mob ran full force toward the wagon loaded with provisions stolen from the Quakers.

Stopping just short of plunder, one bearded, bedraggled soldier called up to the plain-clothed Oliver, now a Captain in the army. "Are you bringing in provisions, mister?"

"I am."

"We're mighty hungry," another man chimed in, deep yearning in his eyes.

Oliver sent a questioning glance to one of the officers who had been trying to subdue the mob. The officer nodded reluctantly, knowing the hardship the men had been facing. Oliver reached back and removed the tarp covering the stash of food. Like a band of monkeys, the men careened onto the bed, grabbing whatever their hands could carry, then scurried off with their prized possessions to their respective huts. One man took a moment to acknowledge Oliver with a nod of his head and a "God bless you, sir."

"So we've fed a few out of thousands," Oliver sighed.

They continued their slow traverse of the camp. Oliver felt Hut shift nervously beside him as they passed a pile of hoofless, frozen horse carcasses piled as high as possible—hundreds of them—their stiffened bodies set rigid and tossed like pieces of timber. Nearby, a woman stooped over a boiling cauldron of horse and cattle hooves, her task to render the oil for lamplight fuel.

Oliver answered Hut's unspoken question. "We ran out of feed for the horses, and the hay's been used for bedding. They'll be buried as soon as we have a thaw." He pulled their rig up to the long log building. "Let's get you signed up," Oliver said to Hut.

"I'm already registered as a minuteman," Gabriel said.

The three of them walked into the massive log structure with several fireplaces strategically placed on its periphery. The room glowed from the fires and was abuzz with activity of men, women and children engaged in whatever tasks were needed. Several groups of women sat in circles, repairing worn uniforms. A few cobblers lent their skills to shoe repair. The trio walked up to the recruiter's desk, where a uniformed sergeant stood and extended his hand in greeting.

"I'm Captain Oliver Tewkesbury, and this is my manservant, Hut. He wishes to enlist in the Army."

The recruiter stood to attention and saluted Oliver. Then he turned and looked Hut up and down. "Where you from, boy?"

"He's from Massachusetts," Oliver responded.

"We don't have a black regiment from Massachusetts," the recruiter replied. "Papers?" he asked Oliver.

"He's my manservant," Oliver said. "I was remiss in bringing his papers with me."

Hut kept his eyes on the ground. Gabriel kept his counsel.

"We'll need to find a regiment for him to serve in. Officers are not allowed manservants, begging your pardon, Captain."

"As I expected," Oliver replied. "What are the black regiments?"

"There's the Rhode Island regiment, but they're in Rhode Island at the moment. He can be in your regiment as an enlisted man, but in separate barracks."

Oliver turned to Hut, "Hut, would that work for you?"

"Yessa," Hut replied.

"Please sign him to my regiment," Oliver said. "He's new to war and I can assist him if he's with me."

"Very well," the recruiter replied as he began to complete the paperwork for Hut's enlistment.

"Last name?"

"We've given him ours," Oliver said. "Tewkesbury."

"Hut Tewkesbury," the recruiter repeated as he wrote out Hut's name. "Please sign here," he said as he dipped his pen into the ink well and handed it to Hut. Hut looked up at Oliver with hesitation, and then marked the document with his "X."

"I can issue you no gear at this time," the recruiter said. "But as soon as we have an available uniform, a rifle and perhaps a blanket, they will be issued. When men leave either because they've passed, or because their enlistment is up, we ask them to leave their blankets behind. So you're on the list."

"I'll show him to his barracks," Oliver said as they turned to leave.

Exiting the building, an agitated Gabriel pulled Oliver aside.

"Have you lost your senses, Oliver?" he asked. "What if this slave's mistress comes looking for him? What if she is found guilty of murdering her husband and the courts start to account for his former owner's assets? You could be in deep trouble with the authorities. It anguishes me that you've put yourself at such unnecessary risk. We've saved the man's life. Isn't that enough?"

"Then I should just as soon have left him by the side of that field," Oliver replied, a bit disappointed at Gabriel's dissention.

Chapter 9

Clutching their satchels, Rebecca, Mehti and Jon Bear stood before the large, elegant brick structure of the Brandywine Village Inn. Smoke billowed from all four of its stately chimneys that rose some 20 feet above the imposing roof line. Unidentified savory aromas wafted from the hearth visible from multi-paned windows that reflected the glow of warmth within. *So warm and welcoming*, Rebecca thought as she watched two British officers make their way to the front door.

"It looks costly," Mehti said.

"Too costly, I'm afraid," Rebecca replied. "It's best we move on. Do you agree, Jon Bear?"

"Yes. We should seek out the tavern. It shouldn't be too far from here."

The streets of Wilmington were busy this time of day with wagons of produce making their way through the city. Businessmen walked the streets deep in conversation or negotiations. Armed British soldiers seemed posted at every corner, keeping a casual eye on human traffic.

"Just keep your eyes to the ground," Jon Bear advised as he took Rebecca by the elbow to steady her footing in the deepening snow.

Within a half mile, they came upon a plain two-story structure not far from the banks of the Christina River and just steps from a stretch of wharf hugging it on the river side. Rebecca stared at the log building that housed one chimney. A few small windows made it difficult to view the interior of the potential accommodation. A rough-hewn sign above the door read, "Buck's Tavern."

Turning to Jon Bear Rebecca said, "We have no choice. With the weather possibly worsening, we need to settle in someplace soon."

Jon Bear opened the tavern door to a flood of raucous laughter and conversation. With a bit of timidity, Rebecca stepped inside, her hand firmly clasping Mehti's. The tavern smelled of grog, whiskey and the sea—clearly a seaman's haven. Rebecca was relieved there were no soldiers to be seen. The fieldstone hearth along the right wall loomed large, its massive cavity containing a crackling fire that heated the entire room. Two large black cauldrons hung from fire cranes, their contents at full boil. Unlike the White Horse Tavern back home in Granville, where every unknown entrant was eyed suspiciously, it surprised Rebecca that no one here took any notice of their coming. *A place of transients,* she thought.

The room at noon was as dark as any moonless night, save for the illumination from the fire. Long tables and benches were at full use and consumed the dining area. A short bar stood on the wall opposite the fireplace, manned by a stout, apron-clad bartender without a hair on his head. He looked up from his task of wiping out the steins lined up on the bar and, spotting his latest customers, waved them over.

"What can I do for you folks?" he asked.

"We are looking for lodgings and a meal," Jon Bear said.

"Sorry, but we only have three chambers upstairs and they're all filled up," the barkeep said, delivering with each word a slight lisp from the gape of a missing tooth. Rebecca became dismayed. While Buck's Tavern was not an ideal place, the thought of trudging through the snow to find other accommodations was daunting. Two men, who were in a heated discussion when the weary trio had entered the tavern, began to tussle with each other as tempers flew.

"Excuse me," the barkeep said as he swung his hand towel over his shoulder and made his way toward the two men, whose fists were raised and about to strike. Although he was short, his stoutness had the impact of a massive ox as he stood between both men and shoved them in opposite directions.

"Enough!" he bellowed. "There's a lady present." Then he turned and resumed his station behind the bar, and the two brawlers skulked off, somewhat relieved to be spared from a fight.

"Surely there must be something you can do for us," Rebecca pleaded. "We traveled here from Connecticut and don't know our way. I've come with my sister and farmhand as my escort to visit a sickly aunt who needs our help," she lied. "But she lives several miles from here, near Valley Forge, and we dare not travel any further in this weather."

"Valley Forge is a good thirty miles from here and mostly uphill. You'll probably need a transport, if you can find anyone willing to take you. It's not an easy hike if you are planning to go on foot, which I do not recommend." The barkeep thought for a moment. "There's an alcove off the pantry—just a hallway, really— where we store goods. You can sleep there if you like, but there's no bed. You'd have to sleep on the floor. You're welcome to it and I won't charge you for it. But you'll have no privacy. I can provide you a basin of water to refresh yourselves."

Rebecca searched Jon Bear's face and, seeing a slight nod, said, "We accept your generosity." Lifting their parcels, she followed the barkeep toward the back of the tavern to a dark area of the building, no larger than six by ten feet, crowded with barrels, sacks and stacked boxes.

"I'll see if I can find some coverlets for you," the barkeep said.

"And can you provide us with a meal?" Rebecca asked.

"We've got bread and beans, if that will suit you. No meat today."

"That will suit us fine," Rebecca said as she previewed the space in the dim light, her immediate concern the likelihood of rats visiting in the night.

The three of them dropped their packs and made their way back to the dining area, where they shared a table and benches with some local seamen who suddenly took note of them. One even nodded in Rebecca's direction, which made her squirm with discomfort. Mehti, who ate eagerly, had been uncharacteristically quiet thus far, this new world of people and places being so foreign to her. They were all grateful for the meal, which was filling and satisfying.

After eating, they returned to the alcove and sat among the stores of goods, contemplating their trip to Valley Forge.

"What do you think Oliver will say when he sees you've come all this way?" Jon Bear asked.

"I hope he will be pleased to see me willing to be at his side."

"And what do you think your father will say?"

"I believe he will be most displeased with me, especially with Mehti along."

As the sounds of the tavern died down well after midnight, the three finally drifted off to sleep from sheer exhaustion. Rebecca dreamed of her father. In the dream, she was a child roaming their newly bought fields in Granville, hand in hand with him as he spoke of his plans for planting the land. In the dream, she felt warm and safe in her father's loving presence.

Mehti dreamt she was stalking squirrels with bow and arrow. There were three in her sights and she had to decide which one to chase.

Jon Bear was about to dream when he was hit over the head with a heavy blunt object that knocked him out cold. Rebecca was awakened by the scuffle. "What is…" she groggily came to, startled by the noise. But her mouth was stuffed with a rag before she was able say another word. She could vaguely make out two men, one who grabbed Mehti, his hand over her mouth. Mehti and Rebecca's panicked eyes locked in the near-darkness for just a moment before Mehti also had her mouth stuffed with a rag. The two were immediately encased in burlap bags that bound their arms to their sides, and were flung over the shoulders of their respective captors. No words were spoken, and all that could be heard were Mehti and Rebecca's muffled cries as their captors exited the building, the rush of cold air penetrating their clothing. They were clearly moving at a hurried pace, most likely to avoid detection and to reach their destination as quickly as possible. The crunch of boots on snow, and the sound of lapping water, was all Rebecca could hear.

"Use the aft gangway," she heard one of the men say. Realizing they were about to board a ship bound for God knows where, she squirmed relentlessly in an attempt to break free. But her captor's arms were too strong and his grip tightened like a vise, making it difficult for her to breathe.

"Stow them in here," she heard a gruff-voiced man say. Next came the creak of a door and the two were thrown to the floor. Rebecca felt her hands being tied at the wrist. "Sleep well, our young ladies. You'll bring good money unless the captain takes a shine to ya," one man said with a laugh. Then came the slam of the door behind them.

Rebecca tried to get their bearings. She struggled to dislodge the cloth from her mouth to comfort Mehti, but was unable to do so. She scooted her body closer to her sister, who whimpered like a wounded animal. The slow rock of the ship and the sound of lapping water overhead told her it was large, much larger than the sloop *Josephine* and, therefore, probably bound for a very distant port.

As she lay on the floor, Rebecca's breath finally slowed and she methodically tried to release her wrists from their bindings. Mehti seemed to settle down as well. Rebecca was uncertain how much time had passed, perhaps a half hour, when she heard the creak of the door again. Panic rushed through her veins again and her heart began to pound in fear. Are we to become slaves at the hands of rogue pirates?

Rebecca felt the burlap bag being pulled from her head; again she was struck with fear as she looked into the eyes of Captain William Treadwell, a knife between his teeth. Shaking her head violently back and forth, afraid of his intentions, she watched him remove the knife as he brought his finger to his lips in a sign to quiet her. He reached down and cut her loose from her bindings as he talked gently to her.

"I followed these thieving varmints from the tavern and waited until they were asleep to board. Luckily, I found you. We need to get the two of you out of here as quickly and quietly as possible."

Rebecca gazed at him in wonder and relief.

"I'm not a bad man, Miss White, just a man to prone to the drink. Perhaps this makes amends." He proceeded to pull the burlap bag from Mehti's head, signaled her to silence and began to cut her bindings as well. Rebecca and Mehti stood, rubbing the pain from their wrists as Captain Treadwell quietly opened the stowage-room door and they tiptoed down the passageway toward a dim light at the stern of the ship. The ship was dead quiet, save for the low moan as wood siding engaged wood dock. Luckily not a single seaman was in view and the gangway remained in place. *They were probably planning an early-morning sail,* Rebecca thought. *This is our only hope of escaping an awful fate.*

The snow had stopped and moonlight glistened on a half foot of the white powder as they crouched down and exited the ship across the same gangway by which they had been brought aboard.

"I must take your leave and head to the *Josephine,*" Captain Treadwell said. "I urge you, quickly to the Buck and Godspeed." He turned and hurriedly trotted off down the waterfront.

Both cloakless, Rebecca took Mehti's hand, "We need to get back to the Buck and find Jon Bear. Hopefully we will be able to gain entrance." The two began to run, encumbered by the snow. Rebecca's worry now was only for the condition of Jon Bear. When they reached the Buck, the tavern door was bolted shut from the inside. Rebecca and Mehti began pounding on the door, yelling for help.

The owner, roused from his sleep, unbolted the door and gave them entry as soon as he recognized them. "What has happened?" he asked.

"We were abducted," Rebecca replied as she and Mehti sped past him and headed for the dark alcove at the back of the tavern. There lay Jon Bear's motionless body, just as they had last seen it.

"Jon Bear," Rebecca called to him as she rolled him to his back and pressed her ear to his heart—a beating heart. "Water, please," she begged the owner as she lifted Jon Bear's head and gently patted his face to revive him. Her hand became immediately stuck to the blood clotted on the back of his head. The owner returned with a tankard of water that Mehti grabbed and instinctively tossed into Jon Bear's face. He moaned, but opened his eyes, then closed them again.

"Lie still," Rebecca said. "You have a head wound we need to tend to." Hearing that, the owner turned to get some swaddling rags. When he returned, Rebecca began to tell him of their ordeal while Jon Bear listened on in a state of confusion, still reeling from his head blow.

"I'm so sorry, miss. I must have forgotten to bolt the back door. But all is secure now and you are safe here."

Rebecca looked down at Jon Bear. "We need to leave at first light," she said. "Do you agree?" Jon Bear nodded slowly as he took a sip from the second tankard of water.

Chapter 10

"Verdammt! Sie verdammten Yankees! Sie sind alle Hunde! Faule Hunde*!" (Damn it! You damned Yankees! You are all dogs! Lazy dogs!)* A rotund Von Steuben yelled in German at the lined-up men, his face crimson with frustration. The men looked about, confused, and turned toward his interpreter, Peter Stephen Duponceau, for an explanation.

Grimacing a bit at the foul language, Duponceau took liberties and told the men, "He asks that you stand erect, hold your right arm out and place it on the shoulder of the man next to you to allow for appropriate spacing." The men did as instructed and managed to get a nod of approval from Von Steuben.

Von Steuben, who arrived at Valley Forge on February 23rd to little fanfare, was nonetheless given full rein by General Washington to train the undisciplined Continentals as he saw fit. The German baron was convinced what was lacking among the troops was a sense of purpose and pride, understandable considering their dire physical condition and the fact that the British had run them out of Philadelphia and beaten them at Brandywine and Germantown. And these particular troops standing before him now were to be his model example as other brigades were required to look on and learn by observing the drilling instruction.

Aside from interpreting drilling instructions, Duponceau had been busy every night translating the military manual written piecemeal by Von Steuben. Once an initial copy had been translated, additional copies were hand printed and distributed to each major who oversaw a brigade. Before learning the drilling and formation exercises described in Von Steuben's manual, Continentals and militiamen had typically marched single file.

Hut and Oliver stood on the sidelines, watching the first drilling practice.

"An act in futility, I would say," Oliver commented, shaking his head as he watched the men.

"I tink I would like to try dat," Hut said with a smile on his face. "Maybe I become a real soldier, too."

"Listen, I have yet to turn in my report to my superior on my little visit to Philadelphia, so I am heading to his office. Keep an eye on those troops," Oliver said as he patted Hut on the back and turned away.

Oliver's commanding officer, Major Wayne Clark, head of Washington's fledgling spy activities, had been eagerly awaiting Oliver's report.

"Enter," Clark bellowed in response to the knock on his cabin door. Oliver ducked under the low cabin heading and stepped into the moderately well-lit room. A blazing fire occupied the fireplace to the rear. Major Clark sat at a makeshift desk tailored from roughhewn slabs of timber. Stacks of papers hid most of his work surface and, upon seeing Oliver, Clark dipped his quill back in the ink well as Oliver saluted him.

"At ease, Captain. I've been waiting patiently for your report, as has his Excellency."

"My apologies, Major, for the delay. It has taken us a few days to get resettled since my return."

"Us?" Clark asked. "And who would 'us' be?"

"I've been joined by a close friend, Gabriel White, a minuteman from Connecticut, and my manservant, who has traveled from Massachusetts," Oliver lied.

"A manservant? I would not have taken you for a slave owner, Captain Tewkesbury."

"Not a slave, Major, but an indentured servant who serves my family."

"Right now, we need every healthy man we can get, so we welcome associates. Now, Captain, what have you to report? Washington awaits my presence as we speak."

Oliver began his summary. "Philadelphia is surrounded by fourteen redoubts that fan out around the city from the north to the south on the west side of the Delaware. Beyond the redoubts there is little activity, save for occasional scouting expeditions. The British like their comforts and disdain winter fighting. It's difficult to tell their numbers exactly, but my estimate would be fifteen-thousand troops, perhaps.

"Loyalists, Quakers mostly, bring wagonloads of food to the city center daily, for which they receive gold in payment. So there is no shortage of food. The wealthiest of the city live in quite a state of grandeur. Balls are held weekly, and many are seen walking the streets in their finery. But all is not well. Wood for heat has been difficult to secure. Furniture of patriots has been burned for heat and there is nary a fence left within the city that has not been set to ashes. And there is not one tree left standing in the city. They've resorted to felling trees on the perimeter of the city, but do so at some risk. The poor have been removed from the poor house, which has been turned into barracks. The poor now reside at Carpenter's Hall, which is woefully inadequate as there are several hundred.

"To pass the winter entertained, aside from weekly balls, they've started a theater company," Oliver smirked and shook his head at the pomposity of it all.

"And what of our prisoners—have they been receiving the food Washington had forwarded for their care?" Clark asked.

"Patriot prisoners are being held at the New Jail on Walnut Street—maybe five hundred of them. Rumor has it that food delivered for our prisoners has instead been given over to British troops. Many have starved and the jail provides no sanitation."

"That's disturbing to hear," Clark responded as he began to mull over options. "I suspect Washington will discontinue the practice of providing stores if the food is just going to feed the British. It's unfortunate more may starve, but we have enough starvation right here."

"What is our count now on able-and-ready-to-serve men?" Oliver asked.

"Somewhere around seventy-seven hundred, give or take a few hundred. We've lost maybe twenty-five hundred men this winter to death and illness. Some may still come around, but that's doubtful," Clark said. "You've done well, Captain Tewkesbury, but we'll need more information. Washington's major concern is when the British might be contemplating an attack this spring. We need to be ready for that event. Do you think you can get back into the city and probe further?"

"It would be very difficult. I am too obvious. I do my spying mostly by night, which makes gathering relevant information almost impossible. I would need to infiltrate, perhaps as a loyalist, to allow my movement about the city. But I will give this some thought, and I do appreciate your confidence in my ability.

"I understand Mrs. Washington arrived during my absence."

"Indeed she has," Clark replied. "She's made it a point to walk among the troops, which seems to buoy their spirits considerably. And Washington's mood has improved markedly since her arrival. I suspect he'll be dining more regularly now. This wretched war has taken its toll on his spirits, as well."

Clark stood up from his desk and extended his hand to Oliver. "I thank you again, and now I must be off to report your findings directly to Washington. And I will give him your regards, Captain."

Major Clark reached for his tricorner and the two men stepped out from his cabin.

"I will be back to you shortly," Oliver said on their parting.

"See that you do."

As the men exited the cabin, they were met with the low mooing of cattle, eighty head, being herded across the middle of the compound, led by Nathanael Greene and several of his men. Ordered to secure meat and staples from the Pennsylvania countryside, they were delivering on those orders.

The drilling men swiftly moved to the side to let the cattle pass as they cheered and applauded, knowing they would finally be fed. Once the cattle moved past toward the slaughtering house, the men resumed their places, an extra lift to their steps. The unseasonably warm weather also seemed to signal a turn for the better.

Chapter 11

After a hearty breakfast of eggs and potatoes provided by the owner of Buck's Tavern, Jon Bear, Rebecca and Mehti bade him farewell and started their hike toward Valley Forge.

"You'll need to head toward Philadelphia on the Post Road, and then turn off to the left to avoid the city. The road from Haverford is what you should seek," the innkeeper instructed. "Like I said, it's about thirty-two miles as the crow flies, but a bit longer on foot."

Rebecca and Jon Bear thanked him for his hospitality and help and, in the early hours of the morning, set out toward Philadelphia, hauling their packs that held a mid-day snack. Their forward progress was slowed by nearly six inches of new fallen snow, but they were determined to make as much progress as possible. Jon Bear had hoped they could cover ten miles on the first day, but he was prepared to stop whenever Rebecca and Mehti felt they could no longer continue.

At first, the girls held hands as they walked along the side of the road, avoiding the muddied wheel ruts where the snow had become a semi-frozen translucent slush. But Mehti's hands were so cold, she eventually let go and withdrew them to beneath her cloak to keep them warm. Jon Bear led the way, head down, about five feet ahead of them at all times, as if pulling them along like a plow horse. *I wonder if we stopped dead in our tracks if he would even notice,* Mehti thought.

Traffic along the Boston Post Road was slight, with an occasional rider on horseback passing them by, along with a few horse- or oxen-drawn wagons, each driver tipping his hat in acknowledgement, a look of curiosity on their faces. Throughout their trek, they encountered no other walkers.

By midday, after several hours of walking in relative silence, they reached an ice-edged creek surrounded by several homes and a few shops, some six miles outside of Wilmington. Jon Bear was pleased at their progress and agreed to stop and rest at a tanner's shop along the creek's edge. The stench from the tanned hides wafted through the air and settled on them like a shroud. Jon Bear could tell Rebecca was tired, so he walked up to the tannery and spoke with what he assumed was the proprietor who stood on the porch preparing a shipment of bundled hides.

"Excuse me, sir. My travel companions and I would appreciate it if we could rest ourselves on your porch and take time for our meal," Jon Bear said. The tanner looked them over and nodded his head, then continued his packing. As they started unwrapping their cornbread and cheese, the tanner offered for them to sit inside and warm themselves by the fire, a welcome invitation.

"What do they call this river?" Rebecca asked the tanner on one of his trips through his shop.

"This is Naaman's Creek, miss," he replied.

"And how far is it to the nearest town?" Jon Bear asked. "We're heading toward Philadelphia."

"That would be Chester, about seven miles northeast of here on the Post Road."

If we sought out Chester, that would be thirteen miles in a day, Jon Bear thought. *That could be difficult, especially with it getting dark around five o'clock and the temperatures dropping.* Fortunately, while it had been quite cold, there was no wind to hamper their progress. And Jon Bear knew the wind was the most life threatening of nature's elements.

With a sudden sense of urgency, Jon Bear made his decision, "Eat quickly," he said. "We need to press on to Chester. If we pick up our pace even a bit, we should get there just after nightfall."

Mehti and Rebecca did as Jon Bear said and quickly finished their meal. The warmth of the fire, combined with their full stomachs, buoyed their strength and spirits considerably. They thanked the tanner as they exited his property and began the second leg of the day's journey, walking at an extended stride.

Again they proceeded in relative silence until, finally, Mehti asked Rebecca a question that continued to weigh heavy on her mind. "Becca, what do you think Father will say when we arrive at Valley Forge?"

"You asked me that once before. It must be plaguing your mind. I dare not think of it, Mehti." Images of her father's rarely seen explosions of anger flittered through Rebecca's mind, causing her to cringe inside.

"So you think he will be angry?" Mehti would not let the subject drop so easily.

Rebecca swallowed hard. "Truthfully, Mehti, I think he will be furious, especially with me for putting you in harm's way."

"But that's not fair," Mehti said. "I came on my own venition."

"Volition. You came on your own volition," Rebecca corrected.

"I was hoping he would be proud of us wanting to help and all," Mehti said.

It was in the middle of this conversation the three of them paused as a wagon pulled up alongside them and came to a halt. A single driver tipped his broad-brimmed hat and smiled down at them.

"Can I give you folks a ride?" he asked. "The nearest town is several miles away."

As always, Jon Bear and Rebecca exchanged glances and, seeing weariness in each other's eyes, nodded.

"We would be very much obliged," Rebecca said, reaching her hand up to the stranger, who hoisted her up on the wagon's bench. Jon Bear walked around to the other side and made his own way up; Mehti followed Rebecca's lead.

Within a few moments, they were all settled in place, headed to Chester and resting their weary and frozen feet.

Rebecca noted the fine quality of the driver's clothing, which led her to believe him to be a man of means. His ascot was fresh and bright white. The jacket that showed from beneath his greatcoat was finely tailored and adorned with silver buttons.

"My name is Thomas Beeson," the driver said. He smiled at them all and shook the reins of his two handsome quarter horses. "Where are you folks headed in the middle of winter?"

Rebecca took great comfort in the jovialness of the man's temperament. Life had been so serious for too long.

Jon Bear hesitated to say anything, giving Rebecca the opportunity to respond. "We seek the road from Haverford," she replied. "Our ultimate destination is just south of Valley Forge, where my sickly aunt has her farm and is in need of our care," she lied, certain this man was a wealthy Quaker and loyalist.

"And from where do you hail?"

"From Connecticut."

The driver fell silent for a few moments and Rebecca held her breath, her first thought being that he would cast them off his wagon, suspected Patriots.

"You are a brave lot to have traveled all this way," he said, then fell silent again.

"I am Rebecca White and this is my sister Mehitable and my escort and our farm hand, Jon Bear," Rebecca said hastily, to fill the void of conversation. Again silence prevailed.

"Perhaps I can be of help to you," he suggested. "My farm is just south of Haverford and my hope is to reach home by dark this evening. You are welcome to spend the night if you like. I'm sure my wife would enjoy the company, as we are childless and she gets lonely when I am off on business. I can accommodate you womenfolk, but Jon Bear, you would need to stay in the barn with my own farm hands."

Jon Bear was concerned about the separation. Since the event on the *Josephine*, he was hesitant to let Mehti and Rebecca out of his sight. But Rebecca followed an intuitive feeling about their gentleman farmer and immediately accepted. "We would be very grateful for your hospitality," she said.

"Very well," he said, smiling at her. "Then we will bypass Chester and head directly to the farm."

Rebecca spent the next few miles admiring the flowing stone walls and wooded areas of the Pennsylvania countryside, which was the last thing she remembered before drifting off to sleep, leaned up against the genteel frame of Thomas Beeson, as Mehti fell asleep against hers.

"Whoa," Thomas called as he pulled his wagon to a stop in the semi-circular drive of his farm. The sudden lack of motion wakened Rebecca and Mehti as they looked sleepily around to see where they were.

Before Rebecca stood the most beautiful, stately home she had ever seen. Made of brick, it stood two stories high with six windows across the second floor and four across the first. Dark green shutters adored each window and candles were lit in the lower four. Two massive chimneys exited the roof, to the left and the right. The house stood on a slight elevation from the driveway and several steps graced with cast-iron railings led to a brass-adorned front door that immediately flew open.

Adelaide Beeson stood in the entryway in her night robe and night cap, her round, pleasant face aglow in anticipation of her husband's arrival.

"Thomas, what have we here?" she asked as she clasped her hands together in delight.

"I've brought some travelers home with me, Addie. I hope you don't mind," Thomas said as they all descended the wagon. "This is Rebecca, Mehitable and Jon Bear." He called to his farm hand to secure the rig and escort the horses to the barn for feed and watering.

With only slippers on her feet, Adelaide swept her well-fed body down the stairs and engulfed Rebecca and Mehti in her arms, as if they were long-lost cousins. "Welcome to Bridlebrook," she said. "Let's get you inside. I'll bet you'd like some tea. And I have some scones left over from our four o'clock." Adelaide was effervescent and, as Thomas had predicted, so terribly pleased to have company.

Rebecca and Mehti looked over at Jon Bear as he followed the ranch hand to the barn, waving a goodbye to them both. As they entered the front hall, Rebecca marveled at the floor tapestry, stenciled walls, elegant draperies, wall sconces and hanging art. It was all so grand!

Adelaide led them to an adjacent sitting room, no less grand, and sat them each down in two overstuffed wingback chairs alongside an ornately carved fireplace encasing a blazing fire. Mehti was spellbound and speechless for a change.

"Martha," Adelaide called to an unseen maid servant, "Put on the water immediately. We have guests."

The three settled themselves in, warmed by the fire; their hostess began asking Rebecca and Mehti where they were from, how they came to be on the road, where were they headed, how long could they stay, who were their parents, how big was their family, what crops did they grow, what was Granville like, and on and on. At one point, Thomas entered the room briefly to excuse himself from joining them, leaning down to kiss his wife goodnight on her forehead.

Finally, after two cups of tea and several scones, Adelaide could see her guests were quite tired and invited them to follow her upstairs to a bedchamber situated above the kitchen, a good source of heat. After washing up in the basin, Rebecca and Mehti climbed into the four-poster bed and huddled under the weight of several quilts. It had seemed ages since Rebecca felt so safe, protected and warm.

Just as she was about to doze off, a slight rap came at the bedroom door and she saw a candle's glow cascade from under the door and across the bedroom floor. "Rebecca, may I come in?" Adelaide asked.

"Yes, please do," Rebecca said as she sat up in bed.

Adelaide entered, a candle in her hand; coming over to the bed, she hoisted herself up and sat on its edge. She looked over at Mehti who was already sound asleep, then smiled at the initials, "MW" Mehti had etched with her fingernail in the window frost.

Normally jovial like her husband, Adelaide's demeanor took on a serious tone.

"We are not bad people," she said to Rebecca. "But we cannot support the war. We are Quakers, as are many in these parts, and it is not allowed."

"Bad people?" Rebecca repeated. "You and your husband are as kind as anyone I have ever met."

The two women clasped hands with a smile. "We respect and love our King," Adelaide added.

"But he has been such a tyrant," Rebecca said. "How can you support someone who has been so oppressive to his own people?"

Adelaide reflected for a moment. "Could you do harm to me?" she asked philosophically. "Because I could never do harm to another person."

"Of course I could not. You are so kind. But if someone else were to do harm to you or people I care about, I would do everything in my power to stop them, even if it meant being physically violent."

"We live in this beautiful place, and yet we are in constant fear. Soldiers steal our livestock, raid our root cellar, burn our orchards; and some of our friends have been put out of their homes. Whether it's Patriots or the British, in war, it's the people who suffer. Don't you see, dear? War is the real oppressor. I wish we had found another way."

Adelaide patted Rebecca's hand. "Now, you get a good night's sleep and we will see you in the morning." She stepped down off the bed and walked toward the door.

"Tomorrow we head for Valley Forge, early in the morning. My father and a very close friend are there," Rebecca confessed.

"I know, dear. You'll have about a day's walk and it's all uphill. The almanac says the day will be mild. Now you get a good night's sleep," Adelaide replied as she exited the room.

In spite of her tiredness, Rebecca's mind continued to imagine and anticipate her reunion with Oliver and her father, now just one day away. She finally drifted off to sleep, the image of his welcoming face bringing her peace and comfort.

Chapter 12

Oliver made it a point every day to make his way to the parade ground, to observe the troops in drill practice. In three short weeks, their countenance had changed dramatically for several reasons. With the coming of spring, a sense of urgency was in the air as it was expected British General Howe would attack Valley Forge as soon as the weather warmed. After all, Philadelphia was only eighteen miles away.

In spite of the potential imminent threat, the men's spirits were high. For the first time since coming to Valley Forge in December, they had a fairly steady diet of beef, thanks to the efforts of General Greene and his master forager. The shad started running in late February and a fish feast provided needed nutrition. In addition, by the beginning of March the weather had become mild and temperate, and those who were able made their way out of their cabins to regularly breathe in some fresh air. The men drilled with their backs more erect, their chests held a bit higher.

What surprised Oliver the most, however, was the impact Von Steuben's discipline had on the men. The initial confusion caused by the language barrier between Von Steuben and the men was fully overcome when it was discovered Von Steuben also spoke French. His German translations hadn't gone very well. A young New York captain, Benjamin Walker, who spoke fluent French, volunteered his services to translate instructions to the men. From that point on, drilling went much more smoothly.

Von Steuben's military manual was now complete and translated, and was being reproduced by hand to share among the captains. Oliver was impressed that Von Steuben not only introduced military drilling and marching procedures, but his leadership philosophy as well. He had read by candlelight just the night before the baron's advice to captains…

> *A captain cannot be too careful of the company the state has committed to his care… His first objective should be, to gain the love of his men, by treating them with all possible kindness and humanity… He should know every man of his company by name and character. He should often visit those who are sick, speak tenderly to them, see that the public provision, whether medicine or diet, is duly administered and procure them besides such comforts and conveniences as are in his power. The attachment that arises from this kind of attention to the sick and wounded, is almost inconceivable.*

Oliver had to admit it. Von Steuben was an inspiration even to him.

As Von Steuben and his aide de camp shouted maneuvers to the men, some six hundred situated in columns in the middle of the parade, a scuffle broke out in the middle of one column, and men were shoving each other and cursing dissatisfaction. Oliver saw in the distance that Hut was among those in the tussle. Walker rushed into the fray, with Oliver not far behind.

"What goes on here?" Walker asked.

"This nigger can't follow a simple instruction," an accosting soldier complained. "He keeps going straight when it's column right, then he goes right when it about face. I'm tired of running into him."

Oliver arrived on the scene and noted that Gabriel, who was two rows back, looked on, but said nothing.

"What's your name, boy?" Walker asked Hut.

"I's Hut."

"Well Mr. Hut, what seems to be the problem? Don't you understand English?" Walker asked.

"Shore 'nuff, when yuse dis close," Hut replied, pointing to his ears.

"Hut, do you have trouble hearing?" Oliver asked.

"Yessir. De massa, he put dem blows to my head as a chile, so I don't always hear de man," Hut said as he nodded toward Walker.

Walker and Oliver shared a glance. "Isn't this your manservant, Captain Tewkesbury?"

"Yes, he is."

"Then why does he speak of slavery?"

"He was enslaved in his youth, Captain Walker. As I had explained, he is a freeman now in my family's employ."

Walker said no more on the subject and Oliver turned his attention to Hut.

"Step out, Hut," Oliver ordered." This may not be the best job for you right now. Let's get you working in the slaughterhouse."

"Yessa," Hut replied in his usual compliant tone.

As they left the field and the men prepared to continue with the drilling, Oliver glanced back at Gabriel, who just shook his head as if in disgust.

Oliver patted Hut on the back, "Mr. Hut, heh? Is that what we should be calling you from now on?" he teased as they headed to the edge of the field. "Why don't you head over to the slaughterhouse and ask for Captain Gibbons. Tell him I sent you to help out in any way you can," Oliver said.

"Yessa," Hut replied and he picked up his step and headed toward the slaughterhouse at the far end of the compound.

Oliver continued to observe the maneuvers and knew the men would be required to fire their muskets in rounds, a tactic often used by the British. A forward row of men would kneel on one knee while a second row of men would stand slightly to their rear. A simultaneous, two-tiered volley of fire on command would send a barrage of shot capable of mowing down any advancing army. As soon as the first and second line of men fired their muskets, they shifted to their right and retreated to the rear through the columns to reload while two subsequent rows of men would advance and continue in the same manner—the front row kneeling, the second row standing and firing over their heads.

The compound had been cleared on the Schuylkill side of the Forge in preparation for this single exercise, which would only be executed once to save gun power and musket balls.

The first volley went off without incident as the men fired, turned and headed to the back of their column away from their firing smoke. As the next rows moved forward to take their firing positions, the men realized their vision was somewhat obscured, walking directly into the path of their predecessors' musket smoke. But they fired their volleys nonetheless, and with adequate success.

As wafting smoke filled the center of the grand parade, Oliver could barely make out three figures standing motionless on the parade's far side near the Gulph Road entrance to Valley Forge. He strained his eyes to make out the stationary figures that stood out among a bustle of activity—perhaps a couple and their child. When the woman lowered the hood of her cloak, her golden-blonde hair flowed free, and it reminded him of Rebecca. Not a day had gone by that he hadn't thought of Rebecca. While he didn't write as often as he should have, he had just penned a letter to her earlier in the week. It worried him that he hadn't heard a word from her in over a month, which was unusual.

Thinning wisps of lingering smoke hung in the air, and Oliver could see the couple and child heading in his direction. He watched them intently, as they appeared to be approaching him specifically. As they came more clearly into view, he realized it was Rebecca, Jon Bear and

83

Mehti. He shook his head, as if to clear away a mirage, and stared across the expanse again, refocusing. Now there was no doubt in his mind, only a flurry of questions.

They met in the middle of the field and Rebecca reached for him, but he held her at bay by her forearms, his eyes searching hers as Mehti and Jon Bear stood nearby.

"Rebecca, what foolhardiness is this?" Oliver asked. "Jon Bear, please explain."

"Oliver, please don't be angry with me," Rebecca pleaded in a flurry of words that could not escape her mouth quickly enough. "And don't be upset with Jon Bear, as I insisted he escort me here to help the cause. I could not stand to sit and wait in Granville as I did last year, to hear if you were alive or dead." Tears welled up in her eyes. "Our coming here has been a risk, I realize, but I would have it no other way." Finally she stood silent, looking beseechingly into his soft grey eyes as if no one else existed in the Forge but the two of them. Even through her cloak, his touch triggered trembles up her arms and across her chest.

Seeing his mood lighten, Mehti rushed up and grabbed Oliver around the waist, hugging him. "I was a stowaway," she said, "so don't be mad at Becca because I came, too."

Oliver's furor quickly abated and he patted Mehti on the head, then taking Rebecca's hands in his, brought them to his lips for a tender kiss. "You don't know what you've gotten yourself into, Rebecca, but, my God, it is so good to see you." The tension from a few moments earlier seemed to dissipate with the smoke.

"Rebecca? Jon Bear?" Gabriel growled from several yards away. The four of them snapped their heads in the same direction and immediately witnessed the fury in Gabriel's questioning eyes as he abruptly came up to them. "How could you, Jon Bear? I should have you flogged!" Gabriel raged. He turned his back to them, stepping away in disbelief, running his hands through his hair, trying to calm himself. Then turning back to Rebecca, "You have no idea the suffering that exists here," he shouted within inches of her face. "Scurvy, scabies, smallpox, typhus, dysentery—death by the thousands," he yelled, quite beside himself with anguish. "Jon Bear, you will return them to Connecticut immediately," Gabriel ordered.

"No, Father. I am an adult and I can make these decisions for myself," Rebecca argued. "I didn't come all this way just to turn around and go back. And you don't know how much we've been through just to get here."

Out of the corner of his eye, Oliver could see his superior, Major Clark, approaching. Gabriel saw him as well and the two men stood at attention and saluted at once, immediately halting Gabriel's rant.

"At ease, gentlemen," Clark said as he looked over the group.

"Is this your family, Captain?" he asked Oliver.

"Sir, this is my farm hand, Jon Bear, and my daughters, Rebecca and Mehitable," Gabriel replied.

"They've just arrived, but their leaving is imminent," Gabriel said as he glared at his daughters.

Major Clark seemed to mull this notion over. He turned to Oliver, "Captain Tewkesbury, might we have a word in private?" He motioned Oliver aside and the two stepped away and spoke in hushed tones. Then the major briskly walked away, back toward his headquarters, and Oliver returned to the group.

They all searched his face eager to learn what information was exchanged. "The major requests that you stay," Oliver said to Rebecca and Mehti. "Apparently he has a service in mind that you can render in our aid. I'm to report to him in the morning to learn the details."

"Be damned!" Gabriel shouted, and he turned and walked away in a huff. Although he hated the idea of his daughters remaining at the encampment, he could not defy a request by the major.

Finally Jon Bear spoke up. "Oliver, I must return to the farm. Jacob cannot manage it on his own, especially with the spring planting coming up. I'll be returning on foot. It should take maybe fifteen days, traveling on my own. I'd appreciate a meal and a night's stay, and then I need to leave in the morning."

"We should get you all a meal," Oliver responded. "Rebecca and Mehti, we need to find a tent for you both. Unfortunately, family members aren't allowed to stay in the cabins. The tents are lined up between the cabins and the hillsides for shelter."

Oliver took Rebecca and Mehti's hands and they exited the parade ground with Jon Bear trailing behind.

"I'm so excited. I'm going to help the war," Mehti said proudly.

"I still can't believe you're all here," Oliver said shaking his head.

Chapter 13

The canvas service tents did indeed command a row nestled between the solders' cabins and Mount Misery that sheltered them from the wind. Unfortunately, it also kept them in the shade most of the day. There, the last vestiges of snow refused to retreat; the rest of the compound grounds witnessed smatterings of spring in the form of tree buds and wisps of green grass.

With spring came the promise of warmer weather, more food and the possibility of less suffering. What also came with spring was a pall of unspoken anxiety throughout the camp—an attack by the British could be imminent. Instead of a reduction in suffering among the troops, they actually suffered more, as the warmer weather proved a breeding ground for germs and bacteria. Washington ordered removal of the daubing between cabin logs, such a necessity in December, to provide better ventilation. Sickness still ran rampant.

Oliver located a vacant tent, midway along the row of tents, perched several inches off the ground and set on split logs, flat side up, that formed a substantial floor. Rebecca stared at a makeshift fire pit that stood just outside the entryway—their only source of heat.

"There's plenty of wood," Oliver said, seeing her concern. "At least we have that." Rebecca nodded in acknowledgement as Mehti made her way inside, already staking out her corner of the tent as if a prized possession. Her unending exuberance amazed Oliver. For Mehti, this was clearly an adventure. Oliver wondered if she would still be so high spirited two months from now. He worried for them both.

Jon Bear stooped down as he entered the tent and, although he could not fully stand up, nodded in approval. "This will suit you both well, Mehti," he said inspecting what would be their living quarters for who knew how long. Jon Bear had served as Mehti's mentor in all things of nature, including how to live in the wild. Rebecca always chided Mehti that she should have been a boy. But Mehti didn't mind. She loved and felt secure in the out of doors and would choose it over the confines of a household. What Rebecca was unsure of now was how Mehti would manage in Jon Bear's absence.

The two of them sat cross legged and Jon Bear began to advise her, as he had always done. With the reverence of a priest bestowing the sacraments, he extended both hands and offered Mehti his sling shot. "I must keep my knife for my walk home," he said almost apologetically.

"Mehti, listen to me," Jon Bear began in his most solemn voice. "Make sure you are in this tent by every nightfall. Creatures of the night will roam and you must not be their prey. There is food here now, but do not hesitate to eat crow. They are plentiful and can sustain you and their spirit will nurture yours. Drink only from upstream. It appears many of the ill here did not heed this advice. Mountain water is best and upland streams here are plentiful. Always haul water in pairs. Take care of Rebecca, and she must take care of you." With each instruction, Mehti gave a nod of acceptance.

The two of them stood and embraced, then returned to Oliver and Rebecca, who were in deep conversation outside the tent as they tended to fire building.

"It is true, Rebecca, Gabriel has not been himself since his arrival. He sought me out in Philadelphia and came upon me being held by a British soldier and saved my life. His arrival there was fortuitous to my mind. We were fortunate to escape the city and make our way back here. But he seems always restless and agitated. He itches to fight, but should save his angst for the battlefield, if and when that time comes. I fear he suffers guilt from the loss of Anna with a death wish of his own." Gabriel regretted that these last words were likely overheard when he turned and saw Mehti standing next to him.

Rebecca immediately changed the subject. "Oliver, I am quite tired. We've been on the road since early dawn with only cheese and bread as our meal along the way."

"I am so thoughtless," Oliver said. "We must get you all some food and water, then you can rest."

No sooner had he spoken those words than Hut approached with two loaves of bread and what looked like dried beef. His questioning look scanned the group then landed on Oliver.

"Hut, these are Gabriel's daughters, Mehitable and Rebecca, and his farmhand, Jon Bear." Turning to them all, Oliver continued, "I would like you all to meet my manservant from Brookline, Hut."

Hut handed off the food and shook hands with Jon Bear while Rebecca and Mehti simply nodded. "I did not know you had a manservant, Oliver," Rebecca said. "You never made mention of it."

"Perhaps I am a man of secrets," Oliver jested. "Shall we sit and eat?"

They each found a sawed tree stump to sit on, Mehti making sure to position herself between Hut and Jon Bear. She looked up at both of them and then began her query of Hut. She had never seen a black man up close before and he intrigued her.

"Are you a soldier too, Hut?" Mehti asked.

"Yes, miss," Hut replied, smiling down at Mehti.

"Do you like being at Valley Forge?"

"Yes, miss, I's shore do."

"Do you know how to hunt?"

"Mehti, really!" Rebecca scolded. "I am sure Hut does not want to spend his afternoon answering all your questions. My apologies Hut, Mehti is a precocious child who does not always know her place."

Mehti just shrugged, smiling up at Hut, and Hut smiled back. And in what seemed to Rebecca to be an instant, a bond formed between the two, Hut becoming a Jon Bear replacement, perhaps.

Rebecca shifted her attention to Oliver. "Oliver, in what ways may we be of help to the cause, now that we are here?"

"There are many possibilities," Oliver replied. "You can take up the laundry chore and mending of uniforms. That requires hauling the water from the Schuylkill up to the encampment. No washing is allowed in the river, as it's our water source. There's cooking, mostly for the officers. The enlisted do their own cooking. Generally each cook is assigned fourteen to twenty-one officers for meal preparation. Then there's nursing, which is very much in demand."

"I shall do nursing," Rebecca immediately interrupted.

"The suffering is great here, Rebecca. I don't know if that is a wise idea. Once patients are well enough to travel, they are sent to farm hospitals west of here." Oliver said a bit anxiously.

"Oliver, I have been through the pox, so I would be of most value in that capacity, don't you agree?"

"Yes, but then, what of Mehti? She has not been exposed and I thought the two of you would work together," Oliver said.

"I will help with the laundry," Mehti chimed in.

"The river water is cold, and hauling water is difficult work. I don't advise it," Oliver said.

"Then I shall mend," Mehti said. And Rebecca knew it was true that Mehti held quite a good stitch.

"You'll be compensated," Oliver told them.

"Compensated?" Rebecca said incredulously. "Surely you jest. We are here to do our fair share, to do our duty. We have no anticipation of compensation."

"Perhaps, but you will be compensated a small sum in any event—plus your meals. Believe me Rebecca, it is a pittance for what you will be called upon to do. I will look after you both to my fullest extent," Oliver added after a pause.

"And I am sure Father will keep a close eye on us as well," Rebecca said.

"And me too," Hut said, winking at Mehti.

When they finished their meal, Jon Bear, Mehti and Rebecca retired to their tent, bundling themselves in their bedrolls and cloaks to ward of the cold of the night.

"I will keep the fire going through the night," Jon Bear said. "And I will begin my return home tomorrow."

Rebecca and Mehti slept comfortably their first night in Valley Forge. When they awoke in the morning, Jon Bear was gone.

Chapter 14

Gabriel perched on a rock outcropping along the edge of the Schuylkill, his mind reflecting on the death and destruction that had occurred just one week prior. The horrific, chaotic scene was imprinted on his mind—a haunting image he could not dispel. The overwhelming helplessness that had taken hold of him that morning still lingered now as his glazed stare lay on the churning springtime swell of the Schuylkill.

It was also just over a week since Rebecca and Mehti had arrived at Valley Forge, and his worry for their wellbeing seemed endless. He knew Oliver's cabin was not far from their tent and he would be keeping an eye out for them. Gabriel's own cabin sat about a quarter mile away, but he made nightly rounds to check in on the girls. Unknown to Rebecca and Mehti, their father stayed on and watched over their tent usually until midnight, when he would return to his cabin under starry darkness and collapse on his mat.

And then there was Hut to consider. Gabriel could not for the life of him understand the bond between Hut and his daughters—especially Mehti. From the moment they arrived, Mehti had taken to the Negro as if he were her father. Much to Gabriel's consternation, they could be seen walking hand in hand throughout the compound. And while most people paid it no mind, it riled Gabriel for reasons he could not explain, even to himself. Rebecca had mentioned to her father that Mehti was taking time every evening to teach Hut to read and write. What nonsense was that? But Rebecca seemed enthusiastically supportive of Mehti's efforts, and so Gabriel kept his counsel on the matter.

All these thoughts pressed on him greatly, but none more than the loss of life that occurred in the Schuylkill. At the age of 45, even after seeing the deaths at Cambridge, he was uncertain why this tragedy ate at him as it did. Perhaps it was the senselessness of it all. Perhaps he was just getting old. He could certainly feel his age in the deepening ache of his bones.

At the heart of it, the men were deserters, and some said they got their due. They were local waggoneers, making money off a promise of pay to haul goods from farmers to Valley Forge. The wagon master had assured them it would be no more than an eight-hour day for their trip to the encampment. But once they arrived, they were redirected to continue on to Head of Elk, another fifty-mile trek. The wagon drivers felt put upon and this new development angered them. In the wee hours of the morning, the men decided in protest to head back across the river to Pennsylvania with their goods in tow—all twenty-four wagons. But in the dim pre-dawn light, they missed the shallower ford waters and ran into the dark depths of the turbid Schuylkill, several rigs sucked downstream. Many were able to turn back at the bank and save themselves and their wagons, but many others drowned.

The commotion awakened the soldiers whose cabins were nearest the river, including Gabriel. The men emerged from their cabins, having donned blankets as shawls, and ran to the river's edge to the shrill cries of drowning men. Helpless, Gabriel witnessed the splintering of wagons that could not hold up against the force of the icy river at the deep crossing. He witnessed men desperately trying to cling to whatever they could grasp, only to be swept down, or under, not to be seen again. Strangely, the image that bothered him the most was that of the horses, harnessed to their wagons, struggling to make it to shore encumbered, their eyes wild with panic, their nostrils flared, their legs flailing and heads twisted to distortion. Gabriel could not forget their desperate cries, the panicked cries of terrified animals.

And then, within less than five minutes' time, the river was a quiet roil, as if it had consumed nothing and held no memory of the tragedy it had just caused.

Gabriel and the other men rushed to assist the remaining wagon drivers in turning their rigs away from the river and toward the center of the encampment. Officers came to the scene to investigate, hauling the drivers down from their rigs. Most of the men returned to their cabins as soon as the event was over, with little compassion for those who had attempted desertion, and lost their lives in the process.

Sitting on the rocky knoll overlooking the river, Gabriel struggled with mixed feelings surrounding the event. The senseless loss of life left him despairing for the never-ending cost and suffering of war. And now, with half his family here at the camp, he felt even more strongly the burden of the war and potential for loss.

Gabriel turned from the river and, in a stooped gait, made his way back to his cabin.

Chapter 15

As requested, Oliver reported to the cabin of Major Walker to receive instructions on his next spying assignment. He stood at attention—eyes forward, his mind full of questions—patiently waiting for Walker to address him. Sweat trickled down the back of his neck. The daubing between the logs of Walker's cabin had not yet been removed, and his cabin was quite warm and stuffy. Walker, generally prone to formality, had even removed his waistcoat. After finishing a memorandum he was penning, he finally spoke.

"At ease, Tewkesbury."

Walker stood, and with his hands clasped behind his back, began pensively pacing the floor, his brow furrowed.

"Sir?" Oliver inquired.

"Please have a seat, Captain Tewkesbury," Walker said with a gesture toward a chair opposite his desk. He continued to pace, as if to assure the accuracy of his words before speaking. "I've met with Washington and given him your report on Philadelphia. He expresses his gratitude and appreciation for a job well done."

"Thank you, sir."

Walker continued to pace. "With the coming of spring, his immediate concern is the potential for imminent attack by the British. So it is therefore imperative that you return to Philadelphia and gather more intelligence on their movements and plans." He continued pacing.

"You know Major Walker that I would never shirk an assignment such as this, but entrance into Philadelphia at this time may be particularly risky. I could again gain access under cover of darkness and keep my movement to nighttime activity; but then, it's difficult to gather any pertinent information when the occupants are all in their beds."

"We realize the dilemma, Tewkesbury. That's why you'll be entering the city during daylight hours." He stopped pacing and stared directly at Oliver, who almost gagged when he heard that edict.

"I don't see how that's possible, Major. The city is swarming with British troops, loyalists..."

Walker interrupted, "And you'll be one of them. What we propose, Captain, and what I wanted to speak to you about is your entrance into Philadelphia as a visiting loyalist with his family—wife, daughter and servant. We'd like the four of you to enter the city on a wagon loaded with goods for sale. You'll be outfitted as a loyalist Quaker family using the very wagon you brought here on your arrival."

Oliver began to process Walker's proposal while the major continued.

"I believe the risk will be slight for the woman and child, but their role is critical in camouflaging your true mission. No one will suspect you are an infiltrator. We'd like the wife and child to visit shops and mingle with shopkeepers. You should all visit local taverns, befriend the locals as the loyalists you portray, and eavesdrop without detection. I recommend you send Mr. Hut down

99

to the wharfs to mingle with the stevedores, identify shipments coming and going.

"I cannot deny that there is some risk involved. But his Excellency would be eternally grateful if you accept this assignment. You do have an option to decline, but I hope you will not."

"I wish to discuss your plan with the White family and can provide an answer by the end of the day. Your plan is acceptable to me and I believe it to be viable. I suspect the Whites will be enthusiastic to help the cause in whatever way they can, but I must speak with them first, you understand," Oliver responded.

"Of course."

"You should also know that Mrs. Washington has gotten wind of this assignment and taken a special interest in helping to ensure its success. She wishes to lend the services of her seamstress to assist with the outfitting of the woman and child, to ensure their authenticity. We've identified a Quaker patriot farmer nearby who approximates your size. You're to meet with him to acquire your outfit."

"How soon do you wish us to proceed to Philadelphia?" Oliver asked

"Within the next two weeks. Our hope is that the roads will have dried some by then and make your travel less cumbersome."

At this point in the conversation, Oliver felt he had received his assignment and stood waiting to be dismissed. But Major Walker resumed his pacing.

"There is one other item I should probably discuss with you, Oliver," Walker said with hesitation. "It may be that we provided his Excellency and Mrs. Washington with too much information regarding the social activities of Philadelphia. As you know, Mrs. Washington has always had a keen interest in the morale of the men. She walks the grounds periodically, engaging the men in conversation in an attempt to lift their spirits. She, along with Von Steuben, invite selected troops to their respective quarters for meals and conversation, and so forth." At this comment, he waved his hand in the air in a circular motion, an indication of the frivolity of it all.

"Are we to now have a ball at Valley Forge?" Oliver asked in jest.

"Not quite. But the missus has taken to the notion that if the British can have theater in Philadelphia, then the Continental Army can have theater at Valley Forge."

Oliver started to chuckle at the notion, until he caught a stare of rebuke piercing like daggers from the eyes of his superior.

"Of course, sir," he replied soberly. "Begging your pardon, Major, but a theater? Surely you do not expect me to…"

"I'm sure it may seem a bit eccentric to you, Captain, but I assure you, Mrs. Washington has the troops' best interests at heart and sincerely believes that such a venture will keep them occupied in an activity besides drilling and give them some entertainment to which they can look forward. I admit I'm a bit skeptical as well, but what's the harm in it? You may even want to take part. I understand that Washington has ordered the building of a stage."

"I am no thespian, Major," Oliver replied. "But I agree, it can only do some good. Hopefully, the war will be held at bay long enough for the men to participate."

"And once you return from Philadelphia, we should have a better handle on Howe's intentions," Walker replied.

"I'll get right on my assignment, Major," Oliver said as he stood to attention and saluted.

"Dismissed."

Chapter 16

The marshy area that encircled an inlet along the Schuylkill proved a perfect place for catching pollywogs, and Mehti took every opportunity to tromp there with her new-found friend, Isaiah. Mehti tried to find friends among the girls at the camp, but their only interests were in playing with corn dolls, and Mehti was an adventurer. And so it was Isaiah, just one year younger than she, whose companionship she enjoyed most.

With the coming of spring weather, Mehti and Isaiah spent not one moment in their tents, but lunged from their sleeping places, anxious to complete their chores and find time to scout out the grounds in and around Valley Forge. The river provided the most interesting exploratory jaunts of all. On any sunny day, the two would be seen leap frogging their way across the compound, headed for the river banks.

Isaiah was camped in Valley Forge with his mother, Clara, and older sister. His father, a Continental soldier and a farmer, drilled and marched in Oliver's regiment. His family hailed from the outskirts of York, Pennsylvania, the relocation destination to which Continental Congress escaped when the British occupied Philadelphia the previous fall.

Rebecca discouraged Mehti's forays along the river bank, including the marshy areas. The river was swift in places and Rebecca was concerned Mehti or Isaiah might be swept away with one easy slip on the bank. The marsh was safer, but Mehti would return to their tent, her smock muddied up to her knees.

"Mehti!" Rebecca would scold. "Keep out of the marsh. You have but this one smock and it will not last long if it's to be washed every week."

The river bank was exactly where Hut found the two children. They had ingeniously constructed a net by weaving reeds together and stood in the shallows, each holding a side in the misguided hope of catching a fish.

"Mehti!" Hut called. "De mail is in. We need to go."

Since Mehti had been teaching Hut to read and write, the two had taken on the task of delivering mail to the troops, with Hut responsible for reading off the address of each letter. His ability had improved to the point where Mehti rarely needed to assist him. Hut and Mehti were a welcome sight among the soldiers, who listened every day for a call out of "Mail!" Because of the level of disease existing in the camp, the two were forbidden to enter cabins, but instead bellowed a shout and a non-contagious soldier would exit to retrieve the mail. Mehti often saw Rebecca, one of several camp nurses, within a cabin, tending to a listless body, a mopping rag in her hand, and worry on her face.

While Mehti seemed to thrive in this wilderness, the demands of tending the sick took their toll on Rebecca. Mehti and Hut were always trying to get her to rest and eat to keep up her strength. The only thing that buoyed Rebecca's spirits was her regular visit from Oliver for their evening walks around the campground. Oliver shared with her the events of the day, and she with him, like an old married couple. Gossip ran rampant. When would the British attack? Was it true the French might enter the war? Rebecca shared the names of all who had perished on each day, and on and on.

They were walking the grounds when he spoke to her of Major Walker's proposal that they pose as a Quaker family and enter Philadelphia to gather intelligence. As he spoke, a broad smile crossed his face—*perhaps we will be thespians after all.*

Rebecca wasted no time in agreeing to the plan and was excited to visit Washington's quarters as soon as possible. Her primary concern was for Mehti, who didn't always mind as she should. They couldn't afford to have Mehti act up in the middle of enemy territory. She could possibly give them all away. Some stern coaching would be definitely called for in this situation.

Generally, on a good day, it took Mehti and Hut about two hours to deliver the mail. On some days, inexplicably, there was no mail. On this day, their mail bag was quite full and Mehti was sure there would be no more time to play with Isaiah. Halfway through their rounds, Hut said, "Mehti, I tink this letter is for Rebecca... W... h... i... t... e. Dat be our Becca," he said with a sense of pride.

Mehti gasped and grabbed the letter from his hand, staring at it wide eyed at the same time she corrected his diction. "That's 'think,' Hut, not 'tink'—and 'that,' not 'dat.'" Hut nodded. "We must find Rebecca at once, Hut."

Mehti started running through the camp, quickly poking her head into each cabin in search of her sister. With over two thousand cabins at the Forge, this was no simple task, but she knew the general area where Rebecca worked on the east side of the encampment. Finally she found her exiting a cabin, hauling a pail of waste water. Her smock was soiled and her cap lay precariously on her head as if she had been in a tussle. She seemed so weary. Mehti held out the letter with both hands, "Look, Becca, a letter from Aunt Sarah! You must open it, you must, you must," Mehti exclaimed excitedly.

"I've just lost another one," Rebecca said as she absent mindedly reached for the letter.

"Yes, so sad, but can we open the letter?" Mehti asked with a twinge of insensitivity.

Rebecca put down the pail and turned the letter over in her hands. "I think we need to wait until we can sit down with Father and open it together. It's addressed to me, but I'm sure it's for all of us."

"I'll go find Father right now. Hut, let's go!" Mehti said, and no sooner did the words escape her mouth than they turned and were quickly making their way across the compound in search of Gabriel.

An hour later they all managed to gather at Rebecca's tent. Seated in a circle, Rebecca held the letter in her hand as if a golden amulet. Hut stood behind her.

"Hut, I'm sure you can appreciate this is a family matter," Gabriel said, looking up sternly at Hut.

"Yessir, I be goin'," Hut replied. But it was clear he had hoped to be able to share the news as well.

Gingerly, Rebecca opened the letter and began reading.

March 15, 1778

My dear, sweet Rebecca,

I hope this letter finds you well, and wish I could tell you that all is well here. Jacob and Rachael lost their beautiful Anna to pneumonia just this week, and we have buried her by her grandmother Anna on the knoll in the field. Our little Anna is with her grandmother and the angels now. Reverend Miller has been with us in prayer every day since our loss, as Rachael has been quite beside herself with grief.

Now our concern turns to Rachael, who is again with child just two months, such a surprise, given that she was still lactating. We were all joyous that Anna would have a little brother or sister to play with, but it is not to be. I am very sorry to deliver this sad news. We encourage Rachael to look forward to the blessings of the new child.

I share with you the good news that Jon Bear has arrived in Granville safely, although we have slaughtered a lamb to put some meat on his bones. He's told us of the hardships at Valley Forge and I applaud your courage and strength to have made your way there. Jacob has been working the fields more this spring than in the previous years. We all deal with grief in our own way.

Love to my brother. Please take care of yourselves. Write if you can.

Your loving Aunt Sarah

The group sat in stunned silence. Finally Gabriel stood.

"I'll be back at my cabin," he said wiping his nose. "I will deliver the news to Oliver. I expect to see him this evening," Rebecca said.

Mehti sat and cried for the niece she would never get to play with.

Chapter 17

Rebecca and Mehti stood, holding hands, before the temporary home of George and Martha Washington that stood near the confluence of the Schuylkill River and Valley Creek on the north side of the Forge. Washington was invited by the owner, Mr. Potts, to spend the winter using the home as his headquarters while he graciously relocated to a farm outside of Valley Forge. This would be the second winter Martha spent with her husband since the war began, as it was her desire to be at his side during the harshest time of the year.

The house was not as grand as that of Thomas and Abigail Beeson, but it was beautifully constructed of mortared fieldstone, two stories high, with large multi-pane and shuttered windows.

Rebecca had done her best to make Mehti look as respectable as possible. Her smock had been cleaned and her hair combed and tied. It was Rebecca's understanding from Oliver that they were expected, but she felt a pang of nervousness that held her feet in place as she gazed upon what seemed to be a bustling household. Mehti kept looking up at her sister and finally spoke up to prompt Rebecca. "Well?"

"Mehti, it is imperative that you mind your manners within this household. Do not speak unless you are spoken too. Do not forget to respond with 'yes, ma'am' or 'yes, sir' when addressed. If you feel uncertain, look to me and I will help you with a proper response. Do you understand?"

"Yes, ma'am," Mehti responded.

They walked up the front steps to a modest whitewashed front door that was immediately opened by one of Washington's servants, an impeccably dressed tall, slender Negro slave woman with a friendly face.

"Good morning," Rebecca said. "I am Rebecca White and this is my sister, Mehti." We have come to see the seamstress for our outfitting. I believe we are expected."

The servant gestured for them to enter. "Follow me," she instructed. Rebecca was immediately taken aback by the number of people up and about at so early an hour. The front room into which they entered was high ceilinged, a huge desk at one end with an unknown occupant, head down, busily writing. Her eyes were drawn to a large stone fireplace surrounded by painted wood wainscoting that extended from the wood floor to the ceiling. Mehti noticed the same paneling and wondered if any were secret panels to hidden passageways.

They followed the servant into a sitting room just outside the kitchen, where they were directed to seat themselves. Officers and servants alike scurried throughout the house, some in conversation, others carrying household items. Rebecca had never seen so busy a household. The home smelled of an odd combination of gun oil, tobacco, simmering root vegetables and mud.

Rebecca stood immediately and curtsied when Martha Washington entered the room and, amazingly,

Mehti followed suit. Slightly shorter than Rebecca, Mrs. Washington was dressed in a light-blue day gown and matching shawl tied at the bodice. Her white hair was concealed beneath an equally white cap edged in eyelet. Her plump face was warm and welcoming.

"So you are our brave new recruits," Mrs. Washington said to them.

"Yes, Lady Washington, I am Rebecca White," Rebecca said feeling a bit tongue tied. Mrs. Washington extended her hand in greeting.

"And who might you be?" she asked smiling down at Mehti.

"I am Mehitable Mercy White... ma'am. But you can call me Mehti," Mehti responded in her most officious voice.

"Well, you are both very brave, and the work you are willing to do is so important to my husband and the cause. We will all be quite indebted to you both when you complete this mission," Mrs. Washington said. As she said these words, a young woman carrying a basket of materials stepped up behind her. "This is my personal seamstress, Mathilda. She is German and an excellent seamstress and tailor. She will measure you and ensure you are both properly clothed to convince the most inquisitive British soldier you are a dedicated loyalist Quaker. Isn't that right, Mathilda?"

The seamstress curtsied, "Yes, ma'am."

"I must be off," Mrs. Washington said, turned, lifted her skirts and headed for the nearby stairs. Before ascending, she hesitated and turned back to them.

Addressing Rebecca she said, "Dear, have you even acted in the theater?"

"No, ma'am," Rebecca replied with a blush.

"You should consider it. You'd make a beautiful Julia in our little production of *Cato*," she said. Then she turned away again and made her way up the stairs.

Rebecca and Mehti stood as the seamstress began to take their measurements, Rebecca's first. It was just as she was about to measure Mehti that General Washington came striding from the parlor, across the sitting room, heading toward the kitchen. His demeanor was serious, as though deep in thought, his hands clutched behind his back, eyes on the floor. As he passed by, he turned toward them and gave a faint smile that lasted only half a second before he was plunged back into contemplation. Just as quickly as he entered the room, he was gone, like a majestic bald eagle seen swooping to grab a fish, and then is instantly off and away, leaving one to wonder if they ever really saw it at all.

In those brief seconds, Rebecca realized she was holding her breath, paralyzed by his presence without even the wherewithal to return his smile. But she was smiling at the encounter now.

In the meantime, Mehti was busy, head down, watching the seamstress measure her, oblivious to General Washington's presence.

"I think I have all the measurements I need," Mathilda said in her strong German accent.

"How long do you think it will take until we can have a fitting?" Rebecca asked.

Mathilda simply smiled an all-knowing smile. "A fitting will not be necessary. It will fit," she said with complete confidence. "I think it will take me a week to complete your clothing. I will send word to the camp when I am done."

The servant, who had been standing by all the while, motioned for Rebecca and Mehti to follow her as she escorted them to the front door.

After saying their goodbyes, they walked back to their tent and found Gabriel tending the fire.

"Father, what a pleasant surprise," Rebecca said as she kissed him on the cheek. Mehti ran up and hugged him around his slender waist. Gabriel always carried a hearty frame, but like so many at Valley Forge, his diet had been sparse and only in the last month, with beef and fish available, had he begun to gain back some of his bulk.

"Oliver spoke to me yesterday about your mission to enter Philadelphia as a family, along with Hut," he said, wasting no time on niceties. "I told him then, and I will tell you now, I think this unwise. The risks are too great. For God's sake, Rebecca, am I to now lose more of my family?"

"Father, you will lose none of us," Rebecca replied as comfortingly as she could. She realized her father had been suffering a deep sadness since the loss of her mother, one that coming to Valley Forge did not remedy. She didn't want to also see him so worried on their behalf. "We will be quite safe with Oliver and Hut. They are strong, smart and capable men who are quick to act when necessary. You know we will be well protected in their care."

"I fear for Mehti. Do you think she can hold her tongue and play the role of your daughter and not give you all away?"

"We coach her daily and have begun playing our parts here at camp. She addresses me as 'Mother' and Oliver as 'Father' to become accustomed to her role. Mehti will be fine."

"I can hold my tongue when needed. And I am a very clever child, Grandfather," Mehti unabashedly teased.

"So you think you will make a good spy, do you?" Gabriel asked.

"Yes sir."

"Well, we shall see."

Chapter 18

Their new clothes fit perfectly. Oliver, Rebecca and Mehti were transformed into the embodiment of an upper-class Quaker family, their clothes simple, but made of the finest materials available. The wagon was outfitted with goods befitting a well-to-do merchant businessman. Although he wore no stockings, even Hut looked the part of a well-dressed manservant with shoes, clean breeches and tunic. Oliver's pouch jingled with gold.

The "family" sat three abreast in the front of the wagon, while Hut sat in the back amid bails and barrels, his feet dangling off the wagon's end. At the time of their leaving, Gabriel was nowhere in sight, which was unfortunate as Rebecca wanted to say her goodbyes. She noted that it was May 9, 1778 a date she would remember for the rest of her life as the beginning of a series of events that would change her forever.

It suddenly occurred to Rebecca that she had totally missed May first. *How different this May is*, she thought. In years past, Rebecca would have spent May Day morning gathering wild flowers to set in baskets she would then deliver to the front doors of those women of Granville she cherished. Her Aunt Sarah would receive one, as well as Goody Beckham, who had been her mother's midwife, delivering not only Rebecca, Jacob and Mehti, but four stillborn babes as well.

Although they were all a bit on edge over their upcoming covert operation, it was a relief to be leaving Valley Forge. The stench from illness, rotting horse carcasses and butchered beef remains had overwhelmed the entire encampment. Washington had ordered several details to engage in cleanup activities around the camp. The last vestiges of horse remains were being buried, and they passed by more than three hundred workers finishing up the grisly task.

Oliver estimated the trip into Philadelphia would take two days, barring any incidents and assuming good weather. As it turned out, the weather was as perfect as any spring day could offer up, and the roads were quite passable. They stopped at two taverns along the way, where they kept to themselves as much as possible, but continued to role play, even when by themselves. Hut was relegated to sleeping quarters in the barn stalls, just as Jon Bear had been at the Bridlebrook home. He collected his meals at the back kitchen door. Oliver, Rebecca and Mehti supped at each tavern then immediately went to their room, thinking it best not to mingle too much with the locals, uncertain who were patriots and who were loyalists. If they kept to themselves, they wouldn't have to answer questions and declare themselves as either.

Their first night's lodging as a family seemed a bit awkward, but adjustments were immediately made. Oliver slept on the floor in front of the door, a sentinel, while Rebecca and Mehti curled up in the bed.

On the second night, their last evening before entering Philadelphia, they were particularly pensive. Oliver and Rebecca shared their thoughts. Would they be stopped upon entry? Would they be questioned? Where

116

would they stay? Where were the markets to sell their goods? They spent some time rehearsing answers to speculative questions as Mehti listened on before dozing off.

In the morning, after a light breakfast of oatmeal and cornbread, they embarked upon the final leg of their journey, crossing over Grey's Ferry floating bridge to enter the city—the very bridge Oliver and Gabriel had crawled across when exiting Philadelphia two months earlier. At the east end of the bridge, two British soldiers stood reviewing the considerable amount of traffic entering and exiting the city.

"Here we go," Oliver said as the soldier to the left waved them forward. Oliver pulled up his rig, ready to answer a barrage of questions. The soldier simply looked them over, smiled at Rebecca and waved them on.

"Good day to you sir," Rebecca volunteered with an amiable smile. They all breathed a sigh of relief. *Walker was absolutely right about entering the city incognito*, Oliver thought.

"Our first course of business should be to find the marketplace to unload our goods," Oliver said. "We can move around the city lighter after that. My familiarity with Philadelphia is limited, but I venture a guess we should head toward the waterfront."

Philadelphia was a thriving and bustling city, clogged with soldiers, local pedestrians dressed from the wealthiest to the poorest, wagons, carriages and single-horse carts. Rebecca thought the city beautiful with its many regal brick buildings of handsomely designed architecture, the likes of which she had never seen. Almost all of the streets were cobblestone, as were the walkways. What Oliver had told her was true—there wasn't a tree or fence left in Philadelphia.

They found themselves on Front Street traveling north along the Delaware until they came upon a two-block open area where goods were being unloaded from numerous sailing vessels along the wharfs. Oliver pulled the wagon over and secured the reins. Rebecca and Mehti stared to the east, awestruck by the breadth of the expansive Delaware.

"It's almost as big as an ocean," Mehti remarked.

"Wait here," Oliver instructed, and made his way through the crowd to talk to some businessmen and vendors nearby loading goods onto their wagons. Rebecca and Mehti watched as he shook hands and introduced himself to several men in the open market square, who all returned to their wagon as Oliver threw back the canvas and began selling and bartering. In less than an hour, he managed to rid them of all materials, his prices were so low. After all, making a profit was not his goal and the businessmen profited handsomely.

Before departing he asked about lodging in the city. One gentleman suggested they inquire at the Blackwell House on Pine Street.

"Blackwell," Mehti said. "That's Jesse's last name. Or at least it was Jesse's last name."

Jesse Blackwell, a friend, neighbor and hopeful suitor of Rebecca when growing up, had been killed in the Battle of Brooklyn Heights over a year ago. Oliver had witnessed his shooting death. The three of them fell silent for a moment.

As it turned out, the Blackwell House was situated just two blocks from the Old Pine Presbyterian church, Oliver's stakeout location during his first spying foray in the winter. The brick Blackwell House stood as a three-story row building fronting Pine Street, nestled wall-to-wall between buildings of like architecture. Oliver pulled up in front of the building.

"You and Mehti go and make arrangements for our accommodations while Hut and I go find the stables and care for the horse and wagon," Oliver instructed, and drove away.

Rebecca and Mehti entered the Blackwell House and looked around at the sumptuous parlor that greeted guests. The walls were covered with cream-colored wainscoting from ceiling to floor, similar to Washington's quarters, but rimmed with ornate crown molding. To the right, a marble-and-wood, beautifully carved fireplace warmed the room with its glowing flames. Mehti was immediately drawn to it, as she had never seen such artistry in Granville. Scrolls, leaves and curlicues, also cream colored, adorned the perimeter of the fireplace. The head of the mantel was graced with a carved medallion that depicted a bull at its center being brought down by a pair of attacking hounds. For Mehti, it was captivating. Several mahogany chairs circled the room and the walls were covered with oil paintings of beautiful landscapes and people of local importance.

"Mehti, let us sit and wait for Father," Rebecca instructed. Mehti immediately obeyed, in a bit of a daze.

"Yes, Mother," she said.

A gentleman dressed in butler-like attire approached Rebecca from the registry desk in the hallway. "May I help you, madam?" the gentleman asked.

We wish to register for a room, but I prefer to wait for my husband and our servant to register," Rebecca replied.

"And how long will you be staying?" the man asked.

"I am uncertain. Perhaps a few days," Rebecca replied. "My husband is here on business."

"You will be pleased to know we offer servants' quarters, but they are shared."

"Thank you," Rebecca said. "That will be adequate."

Within half an hour, Oliver and Hut entered the front door and registered for the room. Hut carried their luggage up to the second floor, where they were fortunate to have a room that looked out over Pine Street. Hut unloaded their bags, and then went to find his own sleeping quarters located in a lower-level annex off the back of the building. When he returned, they headed into town.

"We'll walk to the center of town and find a tavern for dinner," Oliver said. 'Hut, I'd like you to head down to the docks and find out what you can from the dock hands. Any information could be useful. Mingle and act as though you belong among the workers. We'll come down to the wharf area after dinner and collect you. Keep to the market area where we conducted our business earlier."

"I tink I can get some idea of the goins on down there," Hut responded.

"You mean you 'think' you can get some idea," Mehti corrected.

"Yes, Miss Mehti," Hut replied with a smile before heading toward the docks.

The Sampson & Lion Tavern stood on the corner of Vine and Crown, not far from their hotel. Mehti stared up at the tavern sign depicting Sampson slaying a lion. The tavern sported a canopy along both sides of the building that rounded the corner. As they entered the tavern, they could immediately see it served a mix of clientele of varying ages and economic levels. Men and women, fashionably dressed, sat at cloth-covered dining tables to their right, each table holding not just one, but two lit candles. To their left, they saw a long bar that serviced mostly British soldiers deep in conversation, some rather raucous.

Oliver motioned to an empty table opposite the bar, hoping to overhear the soldiers' conversations. A waitress appeared and they ordered beef stew with dumplings and brown bread.

"Can we order some extra bread for Hut… Father?" Mehti asked.

"Of course we can. Maybe we can order a turkey leg and take that along for him too," Oliver said.

As they were in the midst of their meal, two British soldiers whose voices continued to rise as they were in a serious debate, actually stepped down from their stools and began shoving each other.

"I would be heading back to Britain as soon as they say," the first soldier yelled. "I've had enough of this hell hole of America. They can have it."

"Coward!" The second soldier shoved back. "I'll hear naught of reconciliation. We need to run this rabble into the ground. I'll give 'em their due even if cowards like you want to take the easy road," the second soldier responded. And then he took a swing at his adversary, but missed by several inches and stumbled into Oliver's table. Pulling himself up by the table's edge, he paused on one knee and stared into the beautiful blue eyes of Rebecca, who sat quite startled by the altercation.

"What have we here?" the soldier asked looking up at Rebecca. "A beauty!"

Oliver immediately stood, anticipating that he would need to defend Rebecca against any advances by this drunken sod of a soldier.

"I beg your pardon," Oliver said reservedly. "My family is just enjoying a meal and wishes no trouble. Perhaps you should find your way back to your colleague." Then he helped the soldier to his feet and escorted his swaying body back to the bar.

"Oh, you probably think we should head back to England too," the soldier said obnoxiously as Oliver helped him onto his stool. "You're probably one of those friends of Howe going to his big resignation party.

Enough of parties!" the soldier exclaimed as he raised his mug. "What we need is more fighting!"

"I leave war decisions to the wisdom of our King," Oliver responded. "But I have heard Washington's Continentals are growing in number to maybe fifteen-thousand troops by now," he lied, "so prudence would be wise."

"You're a good man," the soldier said as he patted Oliver on the back. Then he turned to his comrade, all smiles, as if no altercation had occurred. "Shall we have another?"

"I'm afraid I have to cut you off for your own good," the barkeep interjected. "If your superiors come by and see you in this state, you'll be thrown in the jail, so off with you now, and I thank you for your patronage." The barkeep stood opposite them, bracing himself with both hands spread across the bar, waiting for any resistance.

After a moment's hesitation, the second soldier said, "Oh, I guess we'll be going now," and, assisting his comrade, they exited the tavern arm in arm.

Oliver, Rebecca and Mehti finished their meals and made their way out onto the street as well.

"Did you hear that, Oliver?" Rebecca asked. "Howe's resigned! I wonder who will be taking his place."

"And there's some dissention in the ranks," Oliver added. "That's good news for us."

As they headed toward the docks, Mehti held the brown bread and turkey leg wrapped in paper, eager to give it to Hut, whom she was sure would be hungry by now.

Chapter 19

As the trio made their way toward the river, Oliver paused to read a poster nailed to the side of a building. The dung-smeared announcement proved difficult to read in its entirety, but appeared to be a declaration from King George, stating his reasons for pursuing reconciliation talks with the Continentals.

"That explains the furor between our two tavern friends," Oliver said.

The streets of Philadelphia were quite crowded at this early-evening time. Oliver sensed a tension in the city for which he could not reasonably account. Groups of people huddled in discussion at various intersections. Others milled about nervously. There seemed to be a stifled urgency in the pace with which people moved about, as though they were trying to immediately reach some unknown destination.

With the sun setting low to their backs, they came upon the river and headed north toward Market Street, in search of Hut. The waterfront wharf area was constructed of wooden retaining walls that formed the outer perimeter of each wharf, and the number of wharfs was more than Mehti could count. The ships were also too numerous to count.

As they walked along the docks, Rebecca cautioned Mehti, "Do not go too close to the edge. A child could all too easily fall in, as there are no railings here." She gripped Mehti's hand tightly.

They finally spotted Hut opposite the riverbank, positioned for clear views of pedestrians coming and going; he was seated on an upright barrel, whittling a piece of wood. Seagulls swooped, cawed and dove headlong into the water as a fishmonger tossed discarded scraps into the river. At the end of one of the longest piers on the waterfront stood a massive British vessel — the *HMS Porcupine*. The bustle of activity in and around its gangplanks told Oliver it had recently docked. But, just as in the city, the air carried a climate of tension and angst among the people and workers.

The three of them nonchalantly walked up to Hut. Mehti handed him his dinner, which he immediately unwrapped and started to devour.

"Thank you, Mehti," Hut said with perfect diction.

Mehti smiled and nodded; then, looking through the crowds of people at the fishmonger, she noticed a small terrier stationed at his feet, waiting intently for a morsel of fish.

"Dogs eat fish?" Mehti asked.

"A hungry dog will eat just about anything," Rebecca replied.

"So, what have you found out for us?" Oliver asked Hut.

"You see dat boat?" Hut said pointing to the *HMS Porcupine*. "Dat boat bring de message that has everybody so upset," he continued. "Dey say that de French are joining the war with our men. It says de French fleet is coming here to dis place. So de peoples here, dem loyalists, dey want to leave as soon as they can."

126

Mehti interrupted. "Can I go pet the dog?"

Rebecca was so thrilled by the news of the French joining the war, subduing her excitement took all her will. She could barely focus on anything else. "You can pet the dog, but stay where I can see you and come right back," Rebecca said as she watched Mehti cross through the crowd to stoop by the fishmonger to pet the dog. The animal immediately licked her hands at the smell of turkey.

"This is incredibly good news," Oliver said in a hushed tone. "It explains why the city is in such a state." Rebecca nodded her head in agreement. "Did you hear anything else?" Oliver asked.

"Dat's all I heard. De men been unloading dis boat and de peoples been coming here with their belongings, hoping dey can get on de boat and go back to England when it leaves. But so far, de captain, he don't want to take on the people. Dere's too many. So how do you choose?" Hut posed the question.

Rebecca glanced through the crowds of pedestrians, straining to see Mehti. When she finally got a clear view, the dog was sitting in its same spot, yet Mehti was nowhere to be seen. Panic swept through Rebecca's heart. "Oh my God," she exclaimed to Oliver and Hut. "Where is Mehti?" She began swiftly making her way across the street dodging people, wagons and carts to get to the wharf's edge, where Mehti was supposed to be. Oliver and Hut followed her.

"Mehti?" Rebecca yelled, her head spinning to search in both directions of the wharf, and then instinctively looking down at the water. Had she fallen in? Rebecca went straight away to the fishmonger. "Excuse me, but did you see a little girl, about so high?" she asked, holding her hand to chest height. "She was just here, and she's disappeared," Rebecca blurted out in a panic-stricken voice.

"Yes, I saw her, Miss. She was here just a minute ago. She must have just wandered off."

Again Rebecca searched to the north, then the south along the wharf, trying to decide which way to begin her search. She focused her gaze at the people moving along the wharf area, trying to catch a glimpse of a child Mehti's height. She saw nothing.

"Oliver, she's gone!"

"We'll find her. She can't have gone too far. Hut, you check Front Street to the north and I'll check to the south. Come back here as soon as you find her."

Rebecca had already headed out onto the dock and continued to look over the edge, surveying the water as she covered the dock's length at a hurried pace. She craned her neck to look among the people standing alongside the *Porcupine*, its presence reminding her of their abduction at Wilmington. Her mind was racing with all the worst possibilities. Had Mehti been snatched or did her endless curiosity cause her to wander toward something of interest in this busy part of the city?

Mehti was still nowhere to be found. Rebecca hurried back to their starting point on Front Street, turning in place, wondering where to look next, calling out Mehti's name and straining to hear a response to her plea.

"No sign of her," Oliver reported as he joined Rebecca. Hut returned a short time later with the same response.

"Where could she be?" Rebecca asked, expecting no real answer. "We need to find a constable, someone to help us."

"I don't know if that would be wise," Oliver said.

"Not be wise? Not be wise?" Rebecca repeated. "Are you more concerned about our cover than my sister?" she said in an accusing tone, out of sheer angst.

When Oliver responded, "Calm yourself, Rebecca," it reminded her of the frequent times she heard Father express those same words to her tormented mother. She knew she needed to compose herself.

"Hut, you continue looking," Oliver commanded. "Search the different wharfs. Try some of the side streets—anywhere you see activity that might attract an inquisitive child. We'll head back to the room, just in case she's managed to find her way there."

"Yessa," Hut replied and then headed north along the dock area.

His arm across her shoulder, Oliver steered Rebecca back toward the Blackwell House, all the while keeping his eyes alert to any sight of Mehti. Within twenty minutes, they were back to the Blackwell and inquired at the desk.

"Excuse me, sir, but we were about the city and were inadvertently separated from our daughter in a crowd of people. Have you seen any sign of her? "

"She hasn't appeared here, sir, and I've been here all evening."

Oliver and Rebecca shared their look of worry and turned to go to their room. Once inside, Rebecca turned to Oliver. "I don't know if I can bear this, Oliver," she said holding back tears. "Mehti knows her way around the woods, she knows her way around the farm and Granville, but she does not know her way around a city," she said as she made her way to the window. Oliver turned her to him and hugged her.

"Mehti is a strong child who can keep her wits about her. I'm sure Hut will find her," he said with veiled assurance as they both turned and watched from their second-story window as a town crier lit the oil lamps along Pine Street, to ward off the encroaching darkness.

"Where are you, Mehti?" Rebecca whispered as Oliver wrapped an arm across her shoulder and pulled her close.

Chapter 20

The sun shone down on Valley Forge like a sign from God as thirteen blasts echoed across the grand parade. The cannon fire marked the beginning of the celebration of the French Alliance. Word had come two days prior and, within a day, the troops were ready to display their military maneuvers and skills.

Gabriel stood at attention among a regiment of Connecticut militia—poised with his musket—as each brigade, lined up in perfect union, fired rounds in jubilation. Although he kept his head facing forward, his eyes craned to the right as General Washington galloped down the line of troops on his white stallion reviewing the 9,500 men ready and fit for duty. Most of the Continentals were smartly outfitted in full dress uniform, an acquisition that had occurred over the previous few weeks.

A brigadier general shouted to the columns of men, and his cry was repeated down the line: "God Bless the King of France!" and the troops en masse responded in kind, "God bless the King of France!" And then, "Long live the King of France!" And finally, "God bless the European states!" Another cannonade of thirteen rounds was fired, and the men began to proudly execute their drilling skills with perfect accuracy. At the end of the military exercise, with the men still standing at attention and their leader still majestically mounted astride his steed, Washington informed the men they would each receive a gill of rum in celebration. More cheers spread across the valley and echoed from the nearby mountaintops.

Along the north side of the parade, several hundred tables were arranged for an officers' communal dinner that included beef, vegetables and breads. As officers entered the area, adorned in their military finery including powdered wigs, they were greeted by Washington, with Martha at his side. He gratefully shook the hand of every man who passed him. Once all the officers arrived, Washington made his much-awaited announcement that, due to the valiant efforts of Baron Von Steuben, Congress had conveyed upon him the rank and pay of Major General. The men all cheered in unison. The gaiety continued with rounds of toasts to the King of France and to the United American States.

Meanwhile, as the troops dissembled to get their own meals and rum, Gabriel glanced about, taking in all that had been accomplished over their awful winter. *We are ready*, Gabriel thought. *I am ready.* He tried his best to focus on his day-to-day activities and the tasks required of him to continue to prepare for an upcoming battle. But nagging worry for Oliver, and his daughters, never left him. They had been gone now for several days and, while he did not expect to hear anything from them for at least a few weeks, he became more and more anxious as the days went by. And then doubts would overtake his mind. What if they never returned? What if he never heard back from them? He knew as well as anyone the dangers that lurked along the roads between Valley Forge and Philadelphia. Rebecca had told him to have faith that all would be well, but he recognized her as young and oftentimes naïve.

Gabriel could not hold her to fault, however, as he had been all too aware of his own naïveté regarding his wife and the extent of her illness. Although he never spoke of Anna, especially to his daughters, he thought of her daily. He had seen himself as her protector, a role he took on as his marital duty. Anna had been emotionally frail, and everyone who knew her had been aware of that frailty, especially Rebecca and him. But he never thought for a second she would take her own life. Gabriel shook his head, as if to cast out the torment that had plagued his mind for the last year.

As Gabriel headed toward his cabin, he was approached by a captain whom he did not recognize, accompanied by what appeared to be a local woodsman.

"Gabriel White?" the captain addressed him by name.

"Yes sir?" Gabriel responded and stood at attention.

"I am Captain McLane, Allan McLane. I'm filling in for Major Walker, who's been called back home due to a family illness. This gentleman is Isaiah Ruggles, from Richmond," he said turning to the visitor. The bearded man stood about Gabriel's height and was dressed in breeches and boots, a tunic and canvas vest. He guessed the man was also about his own age, 45.

Gabriel gave the man a nod. "How can I help you?" he asked.

"I'm looking for a possible runaway slave who goes by the name of Hut Jumbai. I've been working a murder case in Richmond and believe he may have ties to that case. I suspect he's been through this area, as I've spoken with folks who've sighted him a few months back, maybe twenty miles south of here."

"I told Mr. Ruggles that we have a Hut on our roster—not Hut Jumbai, but a Hut Tewkesbury," the Captain said. "Such an unusual name, I find it hard to believe there is more than one Hut in these parts. I understand that Hut and Oliver Tewkesbury, along with your daughters are on a mission right now in Philadelphia. It's also my understanding they won't be returning for several days. Is that correct, Mr. White?"

"That's correct, Captain."

"Do you know this Hut Tewkesbury, Mr. White? Do you know from where he hails? Perhaps I have the wrong man," the visitor said.

Gabriel hesitated, not sure what he should or should not say. "I am aware of the manservant, Hut, but I cannot account for his origins. Perhaps it would be best if you spoke with Oliver Tewkesbury directly when he returns from Philadelphia. This Hut person you're looking for, you say he may have murdered someone?"

"I didn't say, Mr. White," the visitor replied evasively. "Right now, I just want to find him."

Captain McLane turned to Mr. Ruggles. "You are welcome to stay on here at the Forge until they return. As you can see, we are in a most celebratory mood and, unlike during the winter months, we have many victuals of which you may partake."

Isaiah Ruggles looked Gabriel up and down as if to assess his truthfulness. "I should like to stay and question Captain Tewkesbury immediately upon his return. And I thank you for your hospitality."

"Then please, come and join me, won't you?" Captain McLane gestured toward the festivities and the two men headed to the officers' dining area.

Gabriel let out a breath. *I knew this would come to naught. Maybe Hut has been lying to us all along. Maybe he killed his master,* he thought as he went off to get his canteen and much-needed gill of rum.

Chapter 21

Mehti sat swinging her legs as she delivered another savory forkful of mincemeat pie to her mouth as the grandfather clock in the hallway chimed eight times. She looked around the dining table at the other seated guests gathered in the home of Magistrate Clifton and his wife, Marietta, who sat directly to her right.

Marietta reached her hand down and gently placed it on Mehti's thigh, her face aglow with tenderness, and simply said, "Mehitable, be still child."

"Yes ma'am," Mehti replied, remembering Rebecca's instructions to her before visiting Washington's headquarters at Valley Forge. She tried hard not to think about Valley Forge at this moment because, after all, she was on a spying mission and needed to continue to pretend to be the daughter of a wealthy loyalist Quaker farmer. But the vision of starving, sickly men starkly contrasted to the abundance she witnessed before her. She put it out of her mind and fixed her gaze on the flickering candles on the table—the soft glow of flames on pewter holders.

Mehti examined the room and took in the well-dressed diners sharing the meal; they paid her no mind, as if the household were accustomed to diversity of guests at the dinner table. The men, including the magistrate, wore waistcoats; some men wore powdered wigs. The women wore day dresses just as nice as Mrs. Beckham's back home. Two men, attired in British uniforms, sat opposite her and would occasionally disengage from the general conversation to speak just between themselves. She strained to listen, but their accents and hushed tones made it hard to grasp their conversation. A straight-backed butler slave kept entering and exiting the room, trays in hand as he went around the table, now serving dessert and tea. Mehti had heard of, and even seen, waitresses before, but never a butler.

"Would you like a spot of tea?" Mrs. Clifton asked Mehti.

"No thank you, ma'am," she replied.

Mehti was grateful to be staying at the Magistrate's home. Like the welcoming Quaker farmwife Mehti and Rebecca stayed with on their way to Valley Forge, Marietta Clifton was a childless woman who took one look at Mehti and immediately clasped her hand from the escorting night watchman.

"Seems to have gotten separated from her parents," the watchman said. "Says she don't remember the name of the Inn they're staying at. Found her on Walnut Street." Marietta looked Mehti up and down, noting the quality of her clothing.

"Yep. I figured the same thing," the watchman said, reading Marietta's thoughts as they both looked down at Mehti. "This one isn't any child of the streets."

"She can stay here until we locate her parents," the magistrate's wife said. Then, leading Mehti into her parlor, Marietta began to set Mehti's mind at ease.

"You should not be frightened," she told her. "You will be safe here." She patted Mehti's hand. "'Mehti,' Is that short for Mehitable? I shall call you Mehitable and you may call me Mrs. Clifton. Would you like something to eat? If you wait momentarily, you may join us for dinner."

Mehti could tell that Mrs. Clifton was a genteel lady of some means, with a very tender heart, who probably would have liked to have had a child just like Mehti. At least that's what she liked to think.

After getting swept up in a crowd of people at the wharf, Mehti had been turned around and lost her bearings. She kept to the far side of the street, away from the water's edge, as Rebecca had advised. She called to her sister and Hut repeatedly, but the mass of people and the noise from the wharf made it difficult to hear a response. After searching for some time, it occurred to her that perhaps Rebecca, Oliver and Hut had gone into the city to look for her, so she started walking the blocks of Philadelphia looking up and down the streets she passed, but saw no sign of them. And it was getting dark.

Finally she sat on a doorstep to gather he thoughts. Even though she had no idea where she was or what would become of her, she felt amazingly calm. *This should be no different than being lost in the woods,* she thought as she tried to gauge direction from the sun, which was just setting in the west. *I need to travel east, back to the waterfront.* When she stood up and looked around, a night watchman was passing her by. He bent down to address Mehti eye to eye.

"You look like you're lost," he said.

"Yes, sir," Mehti replied. "We were at the wharf and I got turned around and separated and now I don't know where my parents are," she explained, staying in character.

"You live in the city?"

"No, sir. We came from our farm to sell our wares."

"And what is your name?"

"Mehti Tewkesbury."

"Are you staying in town?"

"Yes sir, but I don't remember the name of the place we're staying. I know it begins with a 'B'."

"The Buckley House?"

"No, sir," Mehti responded, shaking her head.

"Brewster's Place?"

"No, sir."

The night watchman scratched his head, looking both ways up and down the street.

"Well, I have to finish my rounds lighting off these oil lamps. Let me take you to the magistrate's house. Maybe they can help you find your parents. You can't spend the night on the streets. It's too dangerous for a young'un like you."

The magistrate's house was a short walk, only two blocks away. Now Mehti sat at a long wooden table covered with more food and drinks than she had ever seen in her life. The magistrate, who sat at the head of the table hovering over his piece of pie like a vulture about to attack its prey, was rotund enough to indicate that he lived a well-fed life. As the conversation continued, Mehti listened intently.

"Clinton is no fool and he will do right by those of us who have been loyal to the King and to England," one guest offered.

"What concerns me most is pandemonium breaking out in the streets," the magistrate responded. "We cannot afford lawlessness to run throughout the city, exacerbated by a state of panic among the people. The withdrawal must be well planned and executed in a structured and safe manner. We don't need another evacuation as occurred in Boston, what with people tossing their belongings into the harbor. That can't happen here in Philadelphia! A plan—we need a plan! And I need to be informed."

One of the British soldiers responded. "I hesitate to speak out of turn, but I have heard our course is for New York and that Clinton does not want to place a burden on the loyalists of Philadelphia to trek there unaccompanied. Nor can we in good conscience leave them behind. We are gentlemen, after all. Do not say you heard it from me, but he proposes the people of Philadelphia who wish to leave be transported on boats of the Royal Navy, along with their possessions. Of course, there may be limits to how much each may carry."

"And what of the troops?" the magistrate asked.

"Quite simply, they will march to New York," the second soldier replied with smug confidence, as though it would be a stroll along the waterfront. "It is a mere hundred miles," he added.

"Even so, with equipment and wagons, that will be a huge undertaking," another guest put in. "And then there are Washington's troops to consider."

The first soldier smiled broadly. "I assure you, we are adept at watching our flank and rear."

"Do you have a timeframe for our departure?" a guest asked the soldier.

"Again, you did not hear this from me, as it may change. But my connections tell me we'll be marching sometime in June, once we're assured all willing residents have evacuated the city. We need to proceed with some haste as the rumor is the French fleet is about to disembark from their homeland, headed directly for Philadelphia."

"It is a relief to hear the loyalists of the city will be given safe passage," the magistrate chimed in. "But we need protocol in place to avoid chaos, and I will focus my attention on such. But suffice to say, our reeling days are coming to a close." He smiled referring to the myriad of dances and lavish parties they had all recently attended, held in honor of the retiring General Howe. He raised his glass to his guests. "To General Howe!"

"To General Howe!" they responded in unison.

"And to King George!" the magistrate continued.

"To King George!" they chimed in again.

Mehti looked up at Marietta Clifton. "I remembered the name of where my parents are staying. It's the Blackwell House," she said with a smile.

Marietta looked a bit disappointed. "The Blackwell House is not very far from here. We shall have our servant, Huntley, take you there directly after dinner. I am sure they will be so pleased to know that you are safe."

Mehti felt a bit disappointed, too. She liked this warm, safe home a lot better than her tent back in Valley Forge. And she liked Mrs. Clifton and wondered what her life would be like if she had such a mother. Her thoughts turned to her own mother and the sadness Mehti still felt at her mother's suicide. But again, she determined to put those thoughts out of her mind as she stepped down from the dinner table, took Huntley's hand and waved goodbye to Mrs. Clifton and her guests.

Ten minutes later, the slave Huntley and Mehti stood in the lobby of The Blackwell House while the desk clerk headed for the stairs to notify the Tewkesburys of her arrival. But Rebecca came bounding down the stairs before he even exited the lobby, having seen Mehti's arrival, her gaze fixed out the second-story bedroom window.

"Mehti!" Rebecca cried as she swooped her up in an embrace bereft of worry. Thanking the Cliftons' slave, they turned and ascended the stairs to their room.

"Where are Hut and Oliver?" Mehti asked.

"They're still out looking for you, Mehti."

"I'm sorry I got lost, Rebecca. I just got mixed in with all the people. But I have so much to tell you."

"Let's wait until Oliver returns, then you can tell all," Rebecca said giving Mehti another hug.

Chapter 22

The evening at Valley Forge promised to be entertaining as dusk settled in and a cool starry night would further set the stage. *Cato* was to be performed, as requested by his Excellency, and all was in ready. Howe's Strolling Players were rumored to have performed at the Southwark Theater in Philadelphia to the delight of the British occupiers and the angst of theater-shunning Quakers. Lady Washington was pleased that Valley Forge would not be outdone. In his younger years, Washington, who loved the theater, had played a role in *Cato* at William and Mary College in Williamsburg. He was delighted at his choice for the camp's first major production.

Logistics had proven problematic, as the initial stage had been tentatively set up in the baker's shop, a bit crowded and with little seating. But with the coming of warm weather, the subsequent building of an actual stage along the banks of the Schuylkill—with plentiful seating, at least for the officers—seemed perfect.

The mood of the attendees was light hearted, and for good reason. As the weather improved and word spread throughout Pennsylvania, Virginia and New Jersey that the Continental Army was seeking additional recruits, their numbers began to soar. By mid-May the Army's roster of able-bodied soldiers rose from a little over 9,500 to almost 15,000 well-fed, well-trained and adequately clothed eager men who could taste the possibility of triumph over the British Army. Several skirmishes with the British throughout the winter and spring, some successful, others at a draw, proved to be a testing of their mettle and wit. A sense of pride permeated the air.

With the Schuylkill River as a backdrop, the stage was aglow with candle light along its front planks. The first two rows of benches were reserved for senior officers and their wives who had now also joined their husbands at Valley Forge. George and Martha entered first and were first seated, followed by General Nathanael Greene and his beautiful and flirtatious wife, Caty. General Knox arrived shortly thereafter with his more-than-ample wife, Lucy. Almost all of the officers, dressed in their best uniforms, attended. The women were equally elegantly dressed for the occasion. Enlisted men gladly stood at the rear.

The performance was almost flawless. Lacking female actors, the men did their best to play female parts, such as Cato's daughter, Marcia. There was no question that the troops were inspired by the play. In a final scene, Cato's son, Marcus, lies dead in his arms, assassinated by a traitor, and Cato delivers the moving line—

"Who would not be that youth? What pity is it
That we can die but once to serve our country."

At the back of the audience, Gabriel felt a swell of pride along with the others, as he had had a hand in the building of the stage. He too was enjoying the performance. As he scanned the crowd of standees, he caught the eye of Isaiah Ruggles, the man in search of Hut

Jumbai. As their eyes locked, Ruggles began to make his way through the crowd toward Gabriel.

"Mr. White," Ruggles called out on his approach.

"Mr. Ruggles," Gabriel responded with trepidation, certain Ruggles was intent on interrogating him further about Hut.

"Are you enjoying the performance?" Ruggles asked, to make congenial conversation.

"Quite so," Gabriel responded, trying to cut the exchange short.

"I am enjoying it as well," Ruggles responded. Then, "I cannot help noticing, sir, that when in your presence I feel a hard stare, then you inevitably look away. Perhaps there is something you want to tell me about Hut Tewkesbury?" he asked. "You mustn't let it plague your mind."

"I am not plagued Mr. Ruggles. I am merely an inquisitive man and you present an interesting speculation, is all. I feel certain when Captain Tewkesbury arrives, he will be able to answer all your questions adequately," Gabriel responded. Again his own questions went surging through his mind, although he did all within his power to appear neutral and disinterested. Was it possible Hut had lied to them all about his involvement in the death of his master? He suspected it was the case, but he dared not get involved. It was not for him to judge. *God will judge those who, cheat, steal or murder*, he thought.

"Very well. I look forward to their arrival. I bid you a good evening," Ruggles said as he turned and walked back through the crowd.

Gabriel felt his stomach muscles relax, relieved that Ruggles probed him no further. He could only evade this kind of questioning so long, and he looked forward to the day when Oliver, Hut and his daughters would ride across the Schuylkill River Bridge and enter Valley Forge again. But who knew when that would be, or whether they would ever even return. For Gabriel, the gaiety of the evening drifted away as he sullenly walked back to his cabin, serenaded by the lull of marsh peepers.

Chapter 23

Oliver and Hut returned to The Blackwell close to midnight, tired and distraught that they were unable to find Mehti.

"We looked everywhere," Oliver began as he entered the room. Rebecca silenced him with a finger to her lips, then pointed to the bed where Mehti lay, sound asleep.

"Tank God," Hut whispered. Then he waved them a good night and headed to his own quarters.

Oliver enfolded Rebecca in his arms as he looked on at the sleeping spy. "Wherever did she make off to?"

"Let's talk in the morning. I asked her to wait and tell her story when you both returned. I am anxious to hear what she knows. She was apparently taken in by a local magistrate with whom she dined, and then conveniently remembered the name of our hotel. Their servant delivered her here earlier this evening. She is quite the spy."

In the morning, they ate breakfast in their room with Hut joining them, and listened to Mehti relay what she had heard at the magistrate's dinner table.

"Are you quite sure the soldier said the troops would be traveling to New York on foot and sometime in June? Oliver asked.

"Quite sure," Mehti replied confidently while chomping on a piece of cornbread.

"It's admirable of the British to be so concerned for the safety of the locals. But it's going to be quite a logistical nightmare to move all these people out of Philadelphia in an orderly fashion."

"That's what Mr. Clifton kept saying," Mehti said. "I heard him say it at least twice. He's nervous about it actually."

"Evacuating the largest city in the colonies will be no small task."

"Surely not everyone will leave," Rebecca commented.

"It would not surprise me to see most of the fifteen-thousand residents depart with what they can carry. Their prospects for staying are rather dismal, especially for those who have aided the British and benefitted by their presence. They'll likely be tried, convicted and perhaps even hanged or imprisoned. If I were a local loyalist, I would be on the first boat leaving Philadelphia if at all possible."

Rebecca dabbed her mouth with her napkin. "What's next for us on this mission?" she asked with a smile.

"We should continue to make our way around the city. Perhaps we could do some shopping. We've learned so much already, but engaging in casual conversations with locals should glean even more information. I also want to visit the jail on Walnut Street to see if I can find out how our imprisoned troops are faring. It's only a few blocks from here and we can stop in shops along the way there and back."

"And how do you propose to find out how the prisoners are doing?" Rebecca asked. Surely the guards won't simply let you in to see them."

"I'll think of something."

"And how long do you think we'll be staying in the city?"

"No more than a week, I should think."

Immediately after breakfast, the four made their way up Fifth Street toward Walnut, Rebecca holding tightly onto Mehti's hand, not about to lose her again. As they passed by a clothier, Oliver suggested that Rebecca and Mehti browse the shop while he and Hut walked on toward the jail. He was certain the shop would be stocked with British imports of finery that would, at the very least, be worthwhile to view. But he did hand Rebecca a few guineas, in case something caught her fancy. Being a purchaser of British goods would only complement her cover.

Oliver and Hut could smell Southeast Park before they came upon it. The stench of what they thought was rotting butchered meat attacked their nostrils, causing Oliver to cover his nose with his kerchief. The park had been turned cemetery, a square in the city bordered by the jail where it was reported most patriot prisoners were being held. Two men were busily digging trenches on the northernmost corner of the park, several shrouded lifeless bodies stacked behind them awaiting burial.

As Oliver approached the workers, they paused, welcoming a chance to rest on their shovels. Oliver glanced down into the ditch, which at that point measured around five by five feet and four feet deep.

"How many of these vermin can you fit in one of these pits?" Oliver asked the younger worker. "God in heaven sent them to this end. A well-deserved ending, I might add."

"Easy, mate," the man replied, looking up from the pit at Oliver. "Even I have some compassion for these blokes. After all, they're keeping me employed." Then both men burst out in laughter. The younger man blew his nose on a kerchief and continued. "Once you get in this place," he said pointing over his shoulder at the jail, "this is likely the only way you're coming out. Some of the locals sneak food in, but it's a hotbed of sickness in there. Truth be told, I'm thankful to be out here, digging in this fresh air, instead of hauling bodies out of that hell hole."

"Justice it is, I say," Oliver continued. "How many you think you've buried here?"

The grave digger removed his hat and, scratching his head, looked over at his digging partner and replied, "Maybe a hundred or more. Not sure. We don't keep track. I'm just happy to be working." Rested enough, he ended the conversation and returned to his task.

Oliver surveyed the park and noticed that about half of the grounds had fresh-turned soil. "Good day to you gentlemen," he said as he and Hut turned and headed back the way they had come.

The entire city continued to be in a flurry of activity. Rebecca found out from the shop keeper, who intended to stay in the city when the British left, that boats carrying loyalists would be disembarking around the first June, with the British troops starting their march north at mid-month, confirming what Mehti had told them. As for himself, the shopkeeper felt he had nothing to fear, as he was simply a businessman who did not discriminate against either Tory or Whig.

Over the following week, the "Tewkesburys'" strolls along the waterfront evidenced British ships arriving daily as locals tried to secure passage to either New York or England. Each ship's captain made determinations about what could be stowed on board. Often enough, many rejected personal items of furniture were tossed overboard, rather than be left behind for use by Patriots.

After a week of surveillance, Oliver determined it was time to return to Valley Forge. Their exit from the city proved more difficult than their entrance, with so many evacuees making their way to the outskirts in order to disassociate themselves from the occupying British. All knew as soon as the British exited, the Patriots would set up residence again. The exodus reminded Oliver of the time when he, Jacob and Jesse were traveling down Manhattan Island the summer of '76, walking against a wave of loyalists heading toward Albany, fearful of remaining in the path of war.

As with their trip to Philadelphia, the return ride took two days and was uneventful until late the second afternoon; a thunderstorm caused them to pull over earlier than expected. The next day the muddied roads slowed them, but were, fortunately, passable.

When they finally reached Valley Forge, Rebecca felt a sense of coming home after having lived there for so many months. She was excited to see her father and tell him about their exploits in Philadelphia. Oliver was equally anxious to contact Major Walker, to pass along all they had learned about the British and their plans for evacuation of the city.

Upon crossing the Schuylkill Bridge, they were taken aback by a contingency of what appeared to be Oneida Indians seated in a large circle, just west of the encampment entrance. They appeared to be deep in discussion.

"It looks as though we've secured more allies to our cause," Oliver said.

He pulled the wagon up to his cabin, noting that Valley Forge was no less abuzz than Philadelphia. Rebecca and Mehti stepped down as Oliver and Hut began to unhitch the horses. Two men were approaching from the direction of Major Walker's cabin.

"Hut Jumbai?" one of the men exclaimed loudly from across the way.

"Yessa," Hut turned and responded at the call of his name.

"See Captain, it's just as I thought," Ruggles said to Captain McLane as the two approached Hut and Oliver. "Captain, I demand this man be put under arrest," Ruggles continued as he pulled handcuffs out of the satchel slung across his chest.

"What goes on here? And who are you?" Oliver asked as he watched Isaiah Ruggles grab Hut by the wrists and begin to screw on handcuffs linked together by a short chain.

"Oliver Tewkesbury?" the captain queried. "I'm Captain Allan McLane. I've been assigned here in place of Major Walker, who's been called home due to a family emergency. This is Isaiah Ruggles, a bounty hunter in search of Hut Jumbai, who is a suspect in the death of Henry Jenkins of Richmond, his master. We have him registered as Hut Tewkesbury. But he apparently answers to the name Hut Jumbai. Mr. Ruggles has cause to take him into custody."

Rebecca and Mehti looked on, and now Mehti rushed to Hut's side. "Oliver, you have to do something to help him," she pleaded.

"Captain McLane, I've heard this man's story and he is no murderer," Oliver averred. "We took him in and I reviewed his case, have seen his letter of freedom and given him my name."

"His innocence or guilt is not for you to decide," Ruggles snapped at Oliver. "I'll take him back to Richmond and let a jury make that decision." And then with stronger indignation he added, "I was there with the hounds when we found Jenkins buried in his own back yard. I helped dig him up. Now I've got my man!"

"This man is not a fugitive from justice but a soldier in the Continental Army," Oliver pleaded to Captain McLane. "We need every man we can get. And while he has not proven himself on a battlefield yet, he

153

has been indispensable to our efforts. In Philadelphia alone, he performed admirably on our behalf."

Captain McLane seemed to be weighing options in his mind.

"Mr. Ruggles, perhaps a military tribunal held here would fill your requirements to seek justice," McLane suggested.

"But his crime wasn't a military crime. It was a civil crime," Ruggles bellowed. "And what of my bounty?" he asked with irritation.

"Do you want justice, or to fill your pockets?" Oliver asked.

"Many of us are making sacrifices in the war, Mr. Ruggles. I ask that you take my recommendation as your best course of action," McLane said firmly.

Isaiah Ruggles was fuming, but he eventually realized his chances of walking out of Valley Forge with Hut Jumbai as his prisoner were suddenly slim.

"I don't like it, but I'll live with it. But I want this prisoner kept in the jail until we can assemble a tribunal. If you don't lock him up, he'll sneak off the first chance he gets. And I don't want to be chasing him all over the country again."

Oliver, Captain McLane and Isaiah Ruggles all shared a glance.

"Agreed," Oliver said.

"Agreed," McLane chimed in.

"Then I will deliver him to the jail," Ruggles said as he grabbed Hut by the shirt collar and steered him away in the footfalls of Captain McLane while Mehti and Rebecca looked on, their faces fallen with worry.

Chapter 24

Mehti slowly walked in measured steps, the tin bowl in her hand filled to the rim with cool well water. Her friend Isaiah trotted along next to her, forward and back, circling, his flurry of questions disrupting her concentration. She stopped intermittently to answer him, so as not to spill Hut's water.

"I told you, Isaiah, the trial will be any day now."

"But do you think he did it? Do you think he killed his master? Everyone is saying he probably did it 'cause folks like him don't value life all that much. And you know, they'll do anything to get away. He might have killed that man and made his escape. What do you think?"

Mehti stopped for about the third time, her frustration rising. "I know for a fact he is not capable of such a thing," she responded with the conviction she felt deep in her young bones. "You don't know him like I do. He's a good man who works hard and would not hurt a fly, let alone another human being." She resumed her walking.

Isaiah mulled that over for a time. "So if he didn't kill his master, who did?"

"He says the master's wife shot him dead because of his beating on her all the time."

"Well, then why don't they arrest her?"

"I don't know, Isaiah!" Mehti replied with exasperation. "Now you just have to leave me be about this. I'm tired of answering your questions. If you want to

156

know what happened to that man in Richmond, you just have to come to the trial."

"Lots of folks will be there, Mehti."

"So?"

"I'm just saying, it's pretty exciting."

"Isaiah, don't you have some chores to do? Please take your leave. I have much on my mind."

Isaiah stopped in his tracks as he watched Mehti make her way to the jail. "You might be wrong," he yelled at her back.

"I don't think so," she responded, her determination focused on the task at hand.

Like all the other structures at Valley Forge, the jail measured about twelve feet by twelve feet. The only differences were a heavy metal crossbar lodged in brackets that locked the entrance door in place, and the one window just to the left of the doorway contained several vertically spaced bars. Hut shared the space with four other inmates arrested for offenses of attempted desertion, theft of supplies or drunkenness. Hut was clearly viewed as the most notorious prisoner and, as such, was avoided by his cellmates.

"Hut?" Mehti called out, her line of vision just over the bottom of the barred window.

"I's here, Miss Mehti," Hut replied, leaning against the window ledge.

"I brought you some fresh water from the well. It's not as cold now as when I drew it, but I got it here as fast as I could without spilling it."

"You is an angel, Miss Mehti." Mehti turned away when she saw his eyes well up.

The bars on the window were too close for the bowl to pass through, so Hut bent down to line his lips up with the bowl while Mehti stood on her tippy toes and gently tilted it to allow the cool water to pour into Hut's parched mouth. He drank it all without stopping to take a breath, then wiped his mouth on his sleeve.

"Do you know how many days until your trial, Hut?"

"Dere's a major gonna hold the trial. He stopped by and tell me maybe in a day or two. Dere's the war planning dat's takin' up most of dem folks' time. Only Mister Ruggles is in a heap of hurry."

"You scared, Hut?"

"Shore nuff, Miss Mehti. But I has hope that the Lord will be with me, no matter what happens—if I live or if I die."

"I don't believe in that stuff anymore. Not since my mother died. She killed herself, you know. 'How did God let that happen?' I kept asking myself. Why wasn't God watching out for her? So I don't believe that stuff anymore."

"I understand that. But it's the only hope I have. Don't we have to believe in something, Miss Mehti?"

"I believe in you, Hut, and right now that's enough for me," she said with conviction. "Oh, and I believe in Oliver too, and he says all you need to do is tell the truth."

Hut smiled for the first time. "I believe in you too, Miss Mehti, and in Master Oliver. What your daddy say 'bout you not believing in God anymore?"

"He doesn't talk about it since my mother died. We went to church every Sunday, but he never talked about it, so I didn't either." Mehti changed the subject. "They feeding you okay here? Can I bring you anything?"

"Dey's feedin' us good. But I shore wish dey'd clear out that pot more than every three or four days," he said motioning to the chamber pot in the corner of the cell. "With de heat, it kinda takes away a man's appetite." Mehti nodded in agreement.

"I'll be back tomorrow. Maybe I can find a stool."

When Mehti returned to her tent, Rebecca and Gabriel were seated at a shaded table outside their tent, sharing a meal, deep in discussion over the impending conflict.

"We have several options. We could attack Philadelphia right now, while the British are busy organizing their evacuation. We could attack them as they leave the city. Or we could take a more passive assault and attack their flank on their way north. I think we're outnumbered, so the last option is probably a good one. And keep in mind, they'll be traveling with all their cannons and supplies, which should encumber them tremendously," Gabriel said.

He looked up when Mehti approached. "And where have you been?"

"Over to get Hut some fresh water."

"I told you, Mehti, to say way from that jail. The guards will take care of Hut, so don't you worry."

"It's just that it's so hot, I thought he would be thirsty. And he was."

"I don't like you associating with him. There's every possibility he'll be found guilty and be taken back to Richmond in shackles. It's best you distance yourself now."

"But he's not guilty, Father," Mehti said.

"I believe he is innocent, too," Rebecca chimed in.

"That's for the major to decide, not us," Gabriel retorted.

"But Father, you've always taken a stand for what you thought was right. Why are you not willing to stand up for this man? Why do you not believe his story?" Rebecca asked.

"I think him a bit shiftless, is all. And I choose not to discuss this further. Mehti, I am asking you to keep your distance from Hut," Gabriel said angrily as he stood, grabbed his plate of food and headed toward his cabin.

As the sisters watched their father's swift departure, a defiant Mehti turned to Rebecca. "Well, he asked me to distance myself, but he didn't *tell* me to distance myself." She was convinced more than ever that Hut needed her as his ally.

"Watch yourself, Mehti."

Chapter 25

Positioned at a candle-lit table, Hut was grateful for fresh
air. Across from him, Major Jonathan Ridgefield sat at his
own table, impatient for the proceedings to start.
Although the night air proved cooler than the overbearing
heat of Hut's prison cabin, the heat of daytime lingered
into the night. The major fastidiously positioned his
papers, pen and inkwell with a keen sense of orderliness
that, in a strange way, comforted Hut. It was clear the
officer was focused on the task at hand, which gave Hut
confidence the major's efficient and thorough manner
would lean in his favor. Hut had only seen the major one
other time, when he came to the jail to let him know the
timing of the proceedings, another indication of his
thoroughness.

It was early evening when Hut was retrieved by
his captor, Isaiah Ruggles, handcuffed and brought to the
far end of the encampment—for what Ruggles hoped
would be a swift determination in his favor. A daytime
court wasn't possible, as all officers were consumed with
preparing their men for a possible assault on the British.
Soldiers were drilling daily, cleaning their muskets,
portioning and filling gunpowder pouches, and packing
for a potential march.

A small crowd of perhaps thirty or forty onlookers
had gathered, including Oliver, Mehti, Rebecca and
Gabriel. Mehti was pleased her friend Isaiah's prediction
of piqued trial interest had not come to pass, as she didn't

want to see Hut's fate potentially determined by a scornful mob. The mood of the camp was upbeat and one of eagerness. Few had interest in the relatively minor legal event about to take place.

Major Ridgefield asked for quiet and began his task.

"Let us begin these proceedings. First, let me explain this is not a trial, but a hearing, the sole purpose of which is to determine whether Mr. Isaiah Ruggles has just cause to further detain and take custody of Hut Jumbai, known to the Continental Army as Private Hut Tewkesbury. For purposes here we will refer to the accused as we know him militarily: Private Tewkesbury."

At that comment, Isaiah Ruggles mumbled something and squirmed angrily in his seat, which caught the attention of Major Ridgefield.

"Mr. Ruggles, if you have a concern, speak it now!" Ridgefield said with some irritation.

All heads turned to Ruggles as he stood, then thought better of his protest. "None, sir."

The major continued, "Private Tewkesbury is being accused by Isaiah Ruggles of the murder of his former owner, Mr. Jenkins of Richmond, Virginia. Although a hearing, this is considered a legal proceeding. I alone will ask the questions and I alone will make a determination regarding the disposition of the accused. All parties involved in this case are subject to questioning. Anyone wishing to speak to this case may do so only with my permission. And I remind you all to speak the truth as you know it. Anyone who knowingly provides false information will be charged as such and themselves detained. And I want no unsolicited comments from those gathered," he added as he glanced over at Ruggles, then across the small crowd.

The major paused a few moments to allow the audience to grasp the full measure of his authority. Hut felt a sense of confidence that he was in good hands.

"What does that mean?" Mehti asked as she tugged at Rebecca's smock.

"Hush, Mehti. I can't answer all of your questions now. You need to remain quiet, and I need to listen."

"Mr. Ruggles, take a seat," Major Ridgefield began, motioning to the chair at his left. "Please state your accusations based on the facts as you know them. Opinion is of no value in these proceedings."

"Well, it's like I been saying to everyone who will listen. I'm from Richmond and three months ago it was reported to me by a resident of that town that Mr. Jenkins had gone missing, as did his wife and as did many of the slaves he owned. I was asked to assist in a search for them all. My son and I proceeded to the tobacco farm of Mr. Jenkins with our bloodhounds. There was no sign of either Mr. or Mrs. Jenkins anywhere on the property. I spoke with Rose Jumbai, who I found with several of her young children holed up in one of the slave quarters."

"Explain what you mean by 'holed up,'" the major interjected.

"Well, they was just sitting there."

"So they weren't barricaded or restrained in any way?"

"That's right. Just sitting there, weaving baskets. Said they had no idea where Mr. and Mrs. Jenkins went off to. Just about then, one of my hounds started baying and near about tore my arm off. He jerked me to the far side of the back yard, where the dirt had been recently disturbed, and started digging like an animal possessed. It took no time at all before his claws were tearing at fabric and it was clear someone was buried there. My son and I got some shovels and set out to uncover what turned out to be the body of Mr. Jenkins. Now, I didn't know Mr. Jenkins, but folks in Richmond described him as a good man—a God-fearing man. He appeared to have been shot in the chest is all I could tell. That's an awful end to a good man's life.

"I went on back to Rose and asked her where the other slaves were. She said she didn't know, but I could tell she wasn't telling the truth."

"Please stick to the facts, Mr. Ruggles."

"Yes sir. I suspected she wasn't telling me the truth. Can I say that? After all, it was clear she wasn't telling me the truth. She had to know her master had been killed and was buried right there on the property. So I knew she couldn't have been honest with me."

"Please continue."

"My son knew of her boy, the slave known as Hut Jumbai, and he asked about Hut. She got real quiet and wouldn't answer. So I had a murdered slave owner and a missing slave. That's all I needed to know. We took those dogs all over the farm, sniffing for Mrs. Jenkins, and they only picked up her scent in the slave quarters. But there was no sign of her. I suppose he could have taken her and tossed her in the river and nobody would be the wiser," Ruggles exclaimed. "I spoke with the magistrate, who set a bounty on the head of Hut Jumbai, and I tracked him to this place, hiding out in Valley Forge. Now I want to take him back to Richmond, collect my bounty and see this slave go to trial for the murder of Mr. Jenkins." Ruggles nodded his head toward the audience, a gesture of the finality of his story and then vacated the testimony seat.

"Thank you Mr. Ruggles."

"Private Tewkesbury, will you please take a seat," Major Ridgefield instructed.

Hut made his way to the chair aside the major's table, his hands still cuffed in front of him.

"Mr. Ruggles, please remove the handcuffs from the accused," Ridgefield said. "Surely Private Tewkesbury won't be escaping at this moment."

Ruggles grudgingly unscrewed the handcuffs and returned to his seat.

"Now, Private Tewkesbury, please tell us what you know about the death of your former owner, Mr. Jenkins, and any way you may have been involved."

"I helped bury him," Hut said incriminatingly as the audience gasped and Ruggles smugly nodded toward the major.

"Please tell your entire story."

Hut proceeded to slowly repeat the story he had told Gabriel and Oliver the day after they found him curled up in a thicket of the Pennsylvania countryside. Throughout his story, he focused his vision on Oliver and

Mehti, which gave him courage to speak his truth with more conviction. He told how Jenkins had abused his wife for years and how on the last night of his life, she finally protected herself with one fatal gunshot.

"And you say after this happened, Mrs. Jenkins granted your freedom? Is that correct Private Tewkesbury?" Major Ridgefield asked.

For the first time, Hut looked directly at the Major. "Yessa."

Ruggles jumped to his feet. "What proof do we have of that claim? And what right would Mrs. Jenkins have to relinquish the property of her husband?" he called out.

"Mr. Ruggles, take your seat!" Ridgefield commanded with a booming voice. Then turning to Hut, he asked, "Do you have any knowledge of the whereabouts of Hannah Jenkins?"

"No sa. The last time I sees her, she be in her kitchen and my mammy was helping her pack some victuals in a sack. I suppose she was leaving, herself. But I got no idea where she be off to."

"Thank you Private Tewkesbury. You may step down." As soon as Hut stepped down, Ruggles came immediately to his side and cuffed him again.

"Captain Tewkesbury, please take the stand," the Major instructed, and Oliver complied.

In his testimony, Oliver told how he and Gabriel found Hut during their return from Philadelphia in the cold weather of February. He reiterated Hut's explanation of what occurred in Richmond. But then he produced the note Hut had given him from his former mistress, Hannah Jenkins, and read it to the major.

> *Dearest Mother and Father-*
> *This is my slave, Hut, who I grant his freedom and who*
> *I ask that you take in as a hired servant if at all possible.*
> *Your Loving Daughter,*
> *Hannah*

"Let me see that," the major said. "The note looks authentic, but it's not dated. Captain Tewkesbury, how is it that Private Tewkesbury bears your name?"

"I gave it to him freely, knowing he had been freed by his owner, and as is my right to do. There was no intent to deceive in my decision. Since Hut was willing to enter the Continental Army, willing to support our cause, I wanted to give him a sure-footed entrance into the service with a name that provided him protection—not from the law, but from any further slavery. My family are abolitionists and have for decades worked to secure the freedom of those enslaved. Their blood runs in my veins."

"And how have you found Private Tewkesbury's service to the army?"

"Exemplary."

"You may step down, Captain."

Next the major called Gabriel to testify and, like Oliver, he repeated the story he'd heard from Hut. As to be expected, all three stories aligned perfectly. But as to the question, "And how have you found Private Tewkesbury's service to the army?" Gabriel paused. The audience fell silent waiting for his response. Oliver held his breath, worried Gabriel's displeasure over their association with Hut would negatively taint his testimony.

Gabriel looked over at his family and caught the worry on Mehti's face. With some reservation he finally replied, "I find it adequate, sir."

"I have no further questions," Ridgefield said as he gathered his notes. I will sleep on this matter and render my decision immediately after calls to prayer in the morning. Then he rose and exited across the encampment at a quickened military pace. The hearing had lasted until almost 11:00. The exhausted crowd dispersed, and Mr. Ruggles again took possession of Hut, leading him back to jail as Mehti, Rebecca, Oliver and Gabriel looked on.

Chapter 26

Mehti lay quietly on her bedding, listening intently, waiting for Rebecca's breathing to become rhythmic, a sure sign she had fallen asleep. Back home, Mehti had often ventured out in the middle of the night to join Jon Bear at his Indian gatherings, and felt comfortable making her way to the jail to see Hut. She was certain it would be hard on Hut, not knowing his fate until the morning. She just needed to see him to assure him she believed all would be well, and to bring him the food she had stored in her smock at dinner time.

With nary a sound, Mehti rose from her bed, tiptoed to the tent entrance and untied the flap. Within seconds she was outside and racing across the encampment toward the jail, thankful for the light of the half moon. She felt certain that even if she were caught, Rebecca would understand her reasons for venturing out. Her father, of course, would be furious with her. She tried to block his words from her mind, determined to do what she knew in her heart was right.

Mehti approached the same barred jail window where she had visited Hut the previous day to bring him water. She admonished herself for not thinking to bring water again this night. But at least she made it here and would get a chance to see him before he was possibly carted away, never to be seen by her or her family again. Luckily there were no guards posted this late at night.

"Hut," Mehti whispered through the window as she grasped the bars with both hands. She heard some stirring in the cabin.

"Hut," she called again. "It's me, Mehti."

She heard a groan from inside and now knew she had awakened him. Then came his shuffling across the jail floor. Mehti reached into her smock for the food she'd tied up.

"Here, I brought you some food, Hut."

The food was suddenly snatched, and her hand along with it, as her entire arm was pulled through the bars and she was lifted up until only one tiptoe remained on the ground. Mehti screamed out in sudden panic at the unexpected assault.

"Hut?" the inmate who grabbed her whined, mimicking her call. His breath was foul beneath his mustache, his eyes a bloodshot red, and his face a profusion of sweat that glistened in the moonlight. Mehti tried to pull away from his grasp by pressing her body against the wall of the jail, but she could not gain leverage.

"Where's Hut?" Mehti cried out as she struggled.

"Oh, your friend's been scurried off by his captor, that creature Mr. Ruggles, not more than half an hour ago. Wouldn't let the rest of us out. No, that was too much to ask 'cause we ain't got no nice bounties on our heads. So you just missed your precious Hut. But you're here now and you look pretty strong to me. I'll bet you could lift that crossbar and let us all out of here," he growled.

Mehti could tell this inmate was in a weakened state as he seemed to barely have the strength to keep a grasp on her arm with his sweaty hands. Lifting both feet off the ground and pushing again the jail wall, she pulled with all her strength until his hand passed through the bars. Then with all her might, she rose up and bit down on his hand as he cried out, "Blast, you little brat!" and she was instantly released. Losing the grip her other hand had on the bar, she fell on her back to the ground, scooting backward in an attempt to get as far as away from the jail as possible.

"Come back here, dearie," the prisoner called in an appeasing tone.

But Mehti stood and ran as fast as she could, her heart pounding wildly, her thoughts racing. Ruggles had apparently decided not to wait for a decision by the major that could possibly not go in his favor and had abducted Hut to ensure his bounty. She needed to get to Oliver immediately and let him know what happened. Perhaps Oliver could go after them. Surely he would go after them.

Mehti raced across the deserted encampment toward Oliver's cabin at least a quarter mile away. She banged on his door, unconcerned she was disturbing the other officers.

"Oliver! Oliver!" she cried out as she pounded. "Oliver, wake up! It's me, Mehti!" She could not contain the panic in her voice. Within moments, Oliver opened his cabin door.

"Mehti, what is it? Is Rebecca all right?"

"It's Hut. I went to the jail and Mr. Ruggles has taken him. He's gone, Oliver. You have to go and find them," Mehti demanded, her voice pitched higher and higher with every rapid-fire word. Then she started to cry.

"Hold on there, Mehti," Oliver said as he tucked in his shirt and eased his suspenders up over his shoulders. Mehti grabbed his hand, trying to pull him out of the cabin.

"You have to go now! You have to find Hut!" she pleaded.

"Okay, Okay. Just calm down. I need to get someone to help. Go and wake your father."

"No, I can't. He'll be so angry with me. And his cabin is across the camp. Please, can you get someone else to help? We're wasting time."

"Mehti, you get back to your tent, now."

Oliver called back to one of his cabin mates, a burly sergeant under his command whom he knew well and felt he could count on. Within minutes the two were dressed and had crossed over to the stables to secure two horses. Oliver was certain tracking Ruggles on foot would take too long, but on horseback they would have a chance to catch up with him. And he felt sure Ruggles would take the Gulph Road, thinking he had plenty of time to escape on foot, assuming he wouldn't be found out until morning. But Mehti had found about the abduction just after midnight.

By 1 a.m. Oliver and his sergeant were racing across the Schuylkill River Bridge after stopping to ask the guards if they had seen two men exiting Valley Forge on foot, one perhaps under duress. They responded they hadn't. Oliver determined to press on, sure that Ruggles must have found a way to slip by the guards.

The two men galloped away from Valley Forge down the Gulph Road, the moon lighting their way. Within half an hour's ride, Oliver spied two figures up ahead on the road, undoubtedly Ruggles and Hut. One man turned and saw them coming, then shoved the other to the ground and started running.

"Get Hut!" Oliver yelled at his sergeant, then began his pursuit of Ruggles who steered off the main road and into the woods. Oliver followed right behind, but when the underbrush became too thick for passage by horse, he dismounted on the run and chased the bounty hunter on foot, tackling him within fifty feet of having dismounted. Ruggles hit the ground hard, with Oliver landing on top of him. When he tried to get up, Oliver's fist connected with Ruggles' jaw, displacing it entirely.

"Now, that's justice," Oliver said as he picked up Ruggles by his collar and steered him toward his horse. When they reached the road, the sergeant had removed Hut's handcuffs. The sergeant handed the cuffs to Oliver, who immediately placed them on Ruggles.

"We'll happily escort you back to Valley Forge," Oliver told Ruggles. The sergeant hoisted Hut up onto the back of his horse for the ride back and the three of them followed Ruggles, who was ordered to walk on ahead. At a narrows in the road, with swampy thicket on either side, Ruggles careened to the left and leapt into the swamp, running at a clip in the foggy bottomland.

Oliver sat steadfast on his horse.

"Shouldn't we pursue him, Captain?"

"No, Sergeant, let's let this one go. If he makes it out of that swamp, which I expect he will, he'll have some explaining to do to anyone he comes across. He's of no use to the cause, and now there's one less mouth to feed."

When they returned to the encampment, Oliver returned Hut to the jail. "Sorry, Hut, but I need to keep you here until the major makes his determination on your hearing. You've only to wait until morning, a few hours from now, to learn the outcome."

"I thank you, Oliver, for comin' and gettin' me."

"You can thank Mehti for that. She apparently came looking for you and found you'd been abducted," Oliver said as he led Hut through the prison door, then secured the cross bar in place.

"See you in the morning, Hut."

"Yessa."

Chapter 27

Mehti and Rebecca generally did not join the men in morning call to prayers, but on this day, Mehti asked her if they could go, and so they did. Of course her main purpose for going was to run into Oliver at the earliest possible time, so she could find out firsthand whether he had been able to find Hut. As the crowd of soldiers gathered, Mehti and Rebecca wove their way through them until they spotted Oliver, his head bowed, eyes closed, perhaps starting his own prayer.

"Good morning, Oliver," Rebecca whispered.

"Good morning. What a nice surprise," he responded, smiling at Rebecca.

"Were you praying, or sleeping?" Mehti asked impudently. Oliver shushed her. She tugged at his sleeve and he tried to ignore her, as prayers were about to start. She tugged his sleeve again. Finally he leaned down and she asked, "Sorry Oliver, but were you able to find Hut? That's all I want to know and then I'll be silent, I promise."

Oliver nodded. "And we need not speak of this, for your own protection."

Mehti smiled and bowed her head as prayers began. She wasn't really planning on paying much attention, which she was certain was a sin of some sort. But then the chaplain leading the prayers began talking about the campaign and her interest was immediately piqued.

"Within a few days, we will embark on our next campaign and encounter with the British who are evacuating Philadelphia and heading for New York. The march will be difficult and the heat will tax your energies. Know that God will be with you. Keep your faith strong. Hold fast to faith in our capable leadership, and know you are doing God's work to liberate those who seek freedom from those who have chosen to be oppressors."

"What campaign?" Mehti thought. She knew there had been much talk of patriot soldiers attacking the British, but she had no idea any action was imminent.

After prayers were over, the three of them headed to the far end of the encampment, where the results of Hut's hearing would be rendered. When they arrived, several others had gathered, including Gabriel; and Major Ridgefield could be seen walking steadfastly across the compound. Oliver approached the major and began his explanation of Ruggles' absence and the events of the night before.

"I see," Major Ridgefield responded. "Please be so kind as to fetch the prisoner and bring him here to receive my decision."

Oliver turned and headed toward the jail, returning shortly thereafter with Hut. The major was already seated at his table, reviewing his notes.

"Please be seated, Private Tewkesbury." Then, turning to the small audience, the major continued, "An unusual turn of events has occurred. It is claimed Mr. Ruggles attempted in the middle of the night to remove the prisoner. I suspect his intent was to undermine the authority of this military court and to take Private Tewkesbury back to Richmond to stand trial—and to collect his bounty. However, he was apparently foiled in his attempt and has absconded." The major paused for a moment.

"Mr. Ruggles' absence has no impact on my decision. After hearing the evidence presented here, and after testimony from those who came forward yesterday regarding this case, I believe there is insufficient evidence to substantiate the accusation of this soldier on the charge of murder."

Hut looked up at Oliver with relief on his face. Then the major continued.

"However, with regard to the granting of freedom by Private Hut Tewkesbury's mistress, Hannah Jenkins, I confess an ignorance to the law as it pertains to the state of Virginia with regard to her right to grant such freedom. In the state of Pennsylvania, the widow of a slave owner does not automatically assume ownership of the deceased's assets, regardless of his cause of death. The case of law may or may not be the same in the state of Virginia. As such, I cannot make a determination as to the legality of her granting of freedom of said asset, Hut Jumbai. But in this case, General Washington has solicited slaves to join the Continental Army and with his edict, and with Private Tewkesbury's willingness to join the Continental Army, I must assume the law is on the side of granting his freedom, as long as he serves the military. I have hereby rendered my decision, which is final." The major turned to Hut. "Good luck to you, Private

Tewkesbury. You are free to go." Then the major stood, turned and exited the area as swiftly as he entered it, his mind no doubt full of thoughts of preparation for an impending battle.

Oliver jumped up and went to shake Hut's hand. "Hut, I'm so glad for you. We have so much to do and we need every good man." Mehti ran up and hugged Hut around the waist when he stood.

Rebecca shook his hand. "Congratulations, Hut." She looked around for her father, but he was nowhere in sight.

"We all have our jobs to do, so I suggest we put this behind us and start preparing for our march," Oliver said.

"When do you march?" Rebecca said.

"My understanding is that we'll be leaving the same time the British leave Philadelphia. That's slated for June 19th, just three days from now. Women, children and camp workers will be following the troops; but, unfortunately, none will be allowed to ride in wagons. We'll need to pack up your belongings as best as we can to be portable and light enough for you each to carry on your backs."

"Won't we be coming back?" Rebecca asked.

"It's doubtful. There will be an engagement to be sure. Who knows if we'll even survive? If we do, Washington will determine our next move. I suspect we would occupy Philadelphia again. Although I also suspect the city will be left in a shambles." He paused in thought for a moment. "Excuse me, but I have to start preparing my men."

Rebecca stood, dumbfounded, as she looked out across the center of Valley Forge and watched as men began assembling for their morning drills. By 9:00, the temperatures would reach 95 degrees to begin a heat wave that would last almost two weeks.

Chapter 28

The next day, by 7 a.m., the temperature had already reached 85 degrees. Mehti felt so tired. For two days now, she had sewn more than in the previous two months. She couldn't count how many buttons she had sewn onto uniforms, how many split seams she had mended as she helped prepare the army for the upcoming conflict. One would think the condition of a uniform wouldn't matter. But most of the regular army soldiers wanted their uniforms well maintained. Not that it would make any difference in the outcome of a battle, but because they now felt a sense of pride in who they had become under the direction of Von Steuben.

"Mehti, we have to start packing what we intend to take with us," Rebecca said as she entered the tent and saw Mehti lying on her bedroll. "Oliver will be here any minute to advise us."

"I know," Mehti said, her breath shallow, her voice weakened from fatigue.

"Mehti, you need to get up and start packing. We leave first light tomorrow morning," Rebecca said. She glanced down as Mehti rolled onto her back.

Rebecca gasped.

It can't be, she thought. Then she knelt at Mehti's side and saw upon her sister's cheek what was undoubtedly a pustule—the first sign of smallpox. Her mind reeled. How had this happened? They had been so careful! The year before, Oliver and Rebecca had nursed each other through the disease, so Rebecca knew the level of suffering her sister was facing. She also knew that, having had the disease, she was immune from reinfection. She began to weep quietly.

"Becca, what's wrong?" Mehti asked.

"My sweet Mehti, I'm afraid I have some rather bad news for you. Hopefully I am wrong, but I doubt it. I fear you have contracted smallpox, child." Rebecca wept some more and turned away from Mehti.

"But I can't have smallpox," Mehti said. "I have to follow the troops with you in the morning."

"Mehti, your health won't permit it. You will be staying here, and I should stay and take care of you."

"Becca, you have to go. Father and Oliver will be counting on you. They'll need your help. Besides, everyone is leaving."

"I can't leave you here alone, Mehti. You'll need tending. Someone to keep your temperature down with cold compresses, especially in this heat, and to make sure you get the liquids you'll need. I was lucky because I had a mild case. Maybe you'll be lucky too. But how will I know?"

Rebecca could hear Oliver's voice as he and Hut approached their tent. Exiting, she cut their conversation short. "Oliver, I'm quite sure Mehti has contracted smallpox," she said before he could even express a 'Good morning.'

"I don't understand how this could have happened," she continued, looking earnestly at Oliver. "We've been so careful to keep her segregated from those who have been afflicted."

Hut and Oliver shared a glance. Then Oliver pulled Hut aside, out of earshot of Rebecca. "Run to the jail and see if any of your former inmate companions have taken ill. Mehti told me she had to bite the hand of a prisoner who grabbed her hand through the bars. I thought nothing of it at the time. Find out who that was and what is his condition," Oliver ordered.

Hut immediately fled in the direction of the jail. Within twenty minutes he returned. Rebecca and Oliver had hardly moved since he left them, deep in discussion of Mehti's health and the upcoming march. Rebecca was so conflicted on what she should do.

"Oliver, may we speak?" Hut asked to get him aside. "Tobias," Hut said. "He's da sick one. Smallpox. When I gets to da jail, they was removing him to be transported to da hospital up state. Hopefully he'll make it."

"I think it best we don't mention Mehti's visit to the jail the other night. It makes no difference to her condition, and her father would be furious with her if he were to find out. Right now she needs medical attention, not recriminations." Hut nodded in agreement.

Hut motioned toward Gabriel, who was crossing the green toward them. Rebecca rushed to her father and wrapped her arms around his neck, burying her face in his chest. "Father," she sobbed. "It's Mehti. She's contracted smallpox. I'm sure of it."

Gabriel's face fell ashen. "How did this happen?" he asked, then headed directly toward his daughter's tent.

"No, Father!" Rebecca yelled after him. "You're not immune. You mustn't! Step away!"

Gabriel stopped and thought better of his hastiness. Then he called out to Mehti through the tent walls. "Mehti, sweetheart, it's Father."

"Father, I'm so sorry."

"No need to be sorry. You will get well. We will see to it," he said with as much conviction as he could manage. Then he turned to Hut.

"Are you responsible for contaminating my daughter?" he asked Hut.

"No sa. I haven't been sick. I done had smallpox as a child, so I's immune."

"Father, please," Rebecca pleaded. She reached down and grabbed a chunk of charred wood from the cold fire pit. Stepping up to the tent wall, she drew a large 'Q' on either side of the entrance flap: Quarantined. "We have no idea how Mehti contracted the disease. The only concern now is that she has it and she needs care. I am torn between staying here to care for her and going with you, Oliver and Hut on the march. She needs my help, but I also feel it is my place to go with you and Oliver. I don't know what to do."

"Father," Mehti said as she stuck her head out of the tent. "Becca is thinking of not going with you and Oliver. You have to make her go. I will be okay. I can get my friend Isaiah to take care of me."

"You're talking nonsense, Mehti. I think the illness has already taxed your mind," Gabriel told her. "Besides,

I am sure Isaiah will be accompanying his mother in support of his father."

"I knows somebody who might help," Hut said. "I have a close friend, Ruby Tumms, she could care for Miss Mehti. She's had da pox and she's good at taking care of folks." He could see Gabriel and Rebecca were mulling it over.

"I'll go get her," Hut said without waiting for their response.

Within minutes Hut returned with Ruby Tumms at his side—a slight and attractive milk-chocolate woman in her early twenties with a kind smile, her hair tied back under a cap. Ruby bowed a greeting to Rebecca and took her hands. "She be fine wit me, missus. I take good care of her for you. My, I cared for many a sick chile since I was a chile myself. Even them what has the pox."

"Please step in our tent and meet Mehti," Rebecca said. If there were a possibility someone else would be her caregiver until Rebecca returned, it was important Mehti felt comfortable with her.

Their bond was almost instantaneous. "I will go and fetch some cold water from the well," Ruby said.

"Mehti, I am so conflicted over this decision," Rebecca said. "If I go, I need to know that you'll be okay—that you'll be well taken care of until I return."

"Becca, I will be fine. You must go. If you stayed here and something awful happened to father or Oliver, because you were not there to help them, I would feel to blame. Jacob was so fortunate when he lost his arm that he had someone to nurse him back to health. Someone to keep away the infection. If it weren't for Rachael, he could be dead now." Mehti's breath grew more and more shallow the more she spoke.

"Mehti, please get rest now. Ruby will be back soon to tend to you."

Rebecca stepped outside, where her father and Oliver were still discussing the situation.

Rebecca looked up at Oliver, searching his face, knowing she wanted to be near him and her father. After all, that's why she made the arduous journey to Valley Forge, because she couldn't stand sitting home, not knowing whether they were dead or alive, wounded or suffering.

She turned to Gabriel. "Father, what should I do?"

"It is ultimately up to you, Becca." I cannot make this decision for you. I suppose Mehti will be in good hands and there's not much more you could do for her than Miss Tumms could do. But you'll have no idea how she'll be until we all return. If we all return. Can you live with that?"

"I will have to. Mehti and Ruby are getting on well and I just have to have faith that she will come through this."

Chapter 29

At 4:00 a.m. on the morning of June 19, exactly six months to the day they entered, an advanced army of five thousand well-ordered soldiers led by General Charles Lee exited Valley Forge—regimental flags waving, fife and drum corps playing—and marched over the Schuylkill River Bridge headed north to cross the Delaware at Coryell's Ferry above Trenton. The drum cadence was slow, but spirits and confidence were high. Washington had given specific instructions to Lee to scope out the movements of the British Army until Washington and the main army could catch up with them. Lee and his men were to cause their delay as much as possible, and be prepared to fully engage if necessary. Washington and the remaining army departed just one day later.

Meanwhile, a separate single regiment of men, led by Benedict Arnold, marched southeast for Philadelphia to secure the city. Word came by courier that the British had crossed the Delaware into New Jersey, headed for New York in a slower-moving, twelve-mile caravan. Washington had given all armies instructions that daily marches should take place between 4:00 a.m. and noon, so that men and horses could avoid the searing mid-day heat.

Quartermaster Nathanael Greene and his men had spent the previous week setting up depots along Washington's anticipated route, stockpiling food, straw for bedding, water and barrels of vinegar to ward off intestinal disease; and digging latrines. In addition, a company of men spent the prior week felling trees along the anticipated path of the British. Wells were filled with dirt or had their bucket ropes cut; bridges were destroyed. All was in ready.

Rebecca woke in time to join the march, thankful Ruby Tumms had spent the night. She knelt down by Mehti, fast asleep, and noticed her blotchy face was now covered with smallpox pustules. Unfortunately, her diagnosis had been correct. She leaned over to kiss her forehead that generated heat she could feel even before her lips touched it. Mehti was burning up. For a moment, Rebecca began second guessing her decision to leave. Oliver had packed her essential belongings to be as lightweight as possible, and her pack sat by the tent entrance in readiness. She wanted to run to the well and bring back some cold compresses to apply to her sister's forehead. But there was no time. The army had already begun its exodus from Valley Forge. She crawled over to Ruby's straw bed.

"Ruby, please wake up."

"Yes, miss," Ruby said groggily.

"It's Mehti. She's burning up. You need to run to the well with some rags and a bucket and bring her fever down. I have to leave now."

"Yes, Miss Rebecca," Ruby said and rose, exiting the tent.

"Leave the flaps open," Rebecca called after her. "We need a bit of air in here."

Rebecca again knelt down by Mehti, stroking back the damp, sweaty hair from her blistering forehead.

"Please be well, Mehti. Please fight this and be here when I return," she whispered to her sleeping sister.

When Ruby returned, Rebecca hugged her. "I know you will take good care of her, Ruby." Letting go of Ruby, she abruptly turned and ran to join the other camp followers at the rear of the column, tears streaming down her cheeks. Luckily, she would be able to share a tent with other followers if shelter was needed. Rebecca knew many of the five hundred camp followers—wives, children and sisters of the soldiers, a group that had formed its own community during the winter and spring at Valley Forge. They would all need each other's help and encouragement now. Her father, Hut and Oliver were nowhere in sight and she assumed they were marching on up ahead with their companies. Gabriel had stopped by their tent site the night before to say his goodbyes to Mehti through the tent walls.

"Mehti, it's Father. I'll be leaving in the morning. You will be in my thoughts and prayers, Mehti. I know you to be a strong-willed child and that will save you. But I will pray for you daily."

"I will pray for you as well, Father," Mehti strained with her weakened voice.

Coryell's Ferry sat approximately forty miles from Valley Forge, with numerous hills in between. By the time the troops quit their march for the day, they had traveled almost half way, an amazing accomplishment, given the heat and the amount of equipment being hauled—

cannons and wagons loaded with furnishings and additional supplies.

Rebecca took care to drink from her canteen all along the route, as Oliver and her father had instructed. And just as planned, at noon, the army stopped its forward progress and gathered under a grove of trees that provided some shade, most men collapsing to the ground, their energy depleted by the heat. Rebecca also felt dizzyingly weary and was grateful the worst of the day was over, as she mopped beaded sweat from her forehead and forearms. The trees hummed with the buzz of cicadas that reminded Rebecca tomorrow would be the first day of summer. A soldier leading a horse carrying water jugs paused nearby so people could replenish their canteens. Rebecca heard him mention that the temperatures were hovering just below 100 degrees.

"Drink up, get some rest. Might want to pitch a tent in case of rain," the soldier said. "We want to make it to Coryell's Ferry by tomorrow at noon."

"Is there any news of the British army's movements?" Rebecca asked the soldier.

"Understand they're moving mighty slow. Heard tell they took half of Philadelphia with them," he joked. "Some of our advance troops are sharpshooters and been picking them off from the woods along their route. We just had a number of Hessian deserters join up with us. Said they didn't feel like being British pack mules. Of course, we've got quite a few of our own unaccounted for."

Rebecca wondered how trustworthy Hessian deserters would be to the cause. She wanted desperately to see Oliver, but hesitated to venture out among the soldiers who were simultaneously resting and preparing for the next day's march. She also wondered how her father was handling the heat, his 45 years most likely weighing against him in this weather.

Mehti's friend, Isaiah, and his mother, Clara, and sister came by and asked Rebecca if she wanted to share a tent with them. "It looks like there's a possibility of rain," Clara said. "We should make sure we have shelter."

As the two women were setting up their tent with the help of the children, Hut walked up to them.

"You ladies need some help?" While the two women were sweating profusely, Hut showed no signs of suffering from the heat.

"Hut, how is it you are so unaffected by the heat?" Rebecca asked almost jokingly.

"Ah, dis heat ain't nothing compared to Richmond in July," he said as he set the center pole for their shelter.

Rebecca was relieved to see Hut, so she could find out how Oliver and her father were faring.

"Your daddy doing fine, Miss Becca. Oliver, he been busy meetin' with de other officers makin' war plans and such. But I 'spect he be by to see you if'n he can get away. It hard for de officers to get away, cus dey need to keep put for war planning. Don't mean he not thinking of you," Hut added when he saw the sullen look on Rebecca's face. "War is big doings, Miss Becca."

"Are you scared, Hut?"

"I surprised I live dis long. But yeah, I's scared. I think anybody with a lick of sense in dem be scared."

That night the skies opened up to a torrent of rain that lasted several hours. Each thunder clap was so close it shook their tent—the lightning crackled so brightly, it was like daylight. Buffeting gusts of wind caused the tent pole to lean at an angle. The flap ties strained when the wind pushed hard, as if determined to gain entry.

The next morning, on the verge of daylight, it was clear the road was mud. They quickly dismantled the wet tent and Rebecca carried it to a nearby wagon, then gathered up her belongings. Yesterday's dinner had been plentiful, thanks to the stores Greene's men had set up along the way. Rebecca munched on pieces of cheese and bread as the caravan began its forward march, first light witnessing steam rising from the earth like a sauna. Rebecca's mud-laden skirts made walking that much more difficult. With twenty miles ahead of them to make it to Coryell's Ferry, she knew the day would be long and hard for all of them.

Chapter 30

The trek to Coryell's Ferry was long and difficult. The oppressive heat continued, causing much fatigue among the camp followers as well as the troops. Rebecca tried to focus her mind on her father, Oliver, Hut and Mehti instead of the cramps that plagued her calf muscles. It had been quite a while since she had walked such distances, and her body ached in protest.

Twice soldiers on horseback rode past them toward the head of the column, leading Rebecca to believe they were couriers bringing word from either Valley Forge or Philadelphia. It hadn't occurred to her she could possibly get word of Mehti's condition. Several other soldiers and camp followers had been left at Valley Forge, too sick to travel. The most she could ever hope to hear would be word of their general condition. She wondered how she would be able to return to retrieve her sister. In the haste of their decision and preparation to leave, she hadn't even discussed it with her father or Oliver. She certainly could not return there on her own.

As they trudged along the Old York Road about ten miles this side of Coryell's Ferry, they passed a detail of soldiers busy digging graves for two soldiers who had succumbed of heat stroke. Rebecca's first thought was that one of them could possibly be her father. She stifled the urge to run over and see for herself. Both bodies were wrapped in their bedroll blankets, which luckily did not look like her father's. Rebecca resolved in her mind that her father was still safe and trudged onward. How sad that these men never saw battle. How sad that they were buried in a place no loved one would ever find or have the comfort to visit. She felt grateful that her own mother had been buried on the hillock by their house back in Granville, and she could gaze out at her stone every day. The thought made her long for home.

The army reached Coryell's Ferry just after noon and began the lengthy process of crossing the Delaware on two flatboat ferries that could each carry thirty soldiers at a time. The crossing would take all day and into the night and, of course, the camp followers would be the last to disembark. Rebecca touched New Jersey soil well after midnight and proceeded to locate a place to pitch their tent. They had been told the army would not march the next day, to allow them to regain their strength in light of the long day they had just encountered.

After pitching the tent and partaking in a meal of pork and beans, Rebecca freshened up from a bucket of water they all shared. She collapsed on her straw bed, immediately falling into a deep sleep that lasted until the morning sun bore heat down, causing her to wake in a sweat. She exited the tent to a bright, sunny day and the sound of song birds that swooped through the camp area and lit in numerous oaks that surrounded the landing area. Coryell's Ferry was scenic, with rolling hills surrounded by uphill woodlands. A gristmill sat on the edge of the river, its water wheel at full bore; across from that stood a brick two-story tavern that surely had comforted many a traveler. Even at this early hour, soldiers were entering and exiting the tavern, which she had thought would be off limits to them. But knowing what these men had ahead of them, their officers must have opted for leniency with this regard.

The daylight hours were busy with activity—meal preparation first, then much interaction and discussion about the next day's march. Word spread that the British might be headed for either Sandy Hook or South Amboy through Brunswick. She did not envy the heady decisions of the army officers. War councils were being held nearly every day.

Rebecca sat on a slope of grass, eating oatmeal and watching Isaiah play with some other children in a field across the road and marveled at their energy. *Children can be so resilient,* she thought, and that thought buoyed her hope for Mehti's recovery.

Rebecca toyed with the idea of walking through the campsite in search of her father and Oliver, but thought better of it. Instead, she decided to walk to a nearby stream and soak her feet; she ended up wading into the shallows to wash off the dirt that had accumulated on her skirts. The stream was so welcoming, she actually knelt down in the water, allowing its coolness to caress her legs. She splashed the refreshing water onto her arms and face. It was so rejuvenating, given the drudgery of the last few days.

In the afternoon Rebecca walked among the other camp followers, helping them with meal preparation and tending to some who had fallen ill. By evening, after hearing no word from Hut, her father or Oliver, she retired to her tent, ready for the next day's march. Word had spread that on day four of their march, the army was headed for Hopewell, eleven miles away.

No sooner had Rebecca's head lain on her rucksack pillow than reveille sounded. She and her tent mates were now quite adept at putting up and taking down their tent, and they were up, packed and moving in record time. The day of rest had served them well, as the march seemed less taxing than on previous days. The shorter route of the day allowed for a twenty-minute rest midmorning. The temperatures continued to soar into the high 90s as the oppressive heat wave continued. Every day, Rebecca's clothes were soaked through with sweat.

The army arrived in Hopewell and set up camp at the farm of John Hart, an avid patriot who had signed the Declaration of Independence. Accessing his farm proved a bit unusual, as there were no roads leading to it. The army simply traversed fields and ended up camping on land that had been planted with a variety of crops. Rebecca and the other followers pitched their tents among the waist-high corn. Farmer Hart's home was a stately two-story brick structure with numerous windows across the front of the building and an annex off to the left side. Word spread that the army might be staying at the site for two days, depending on the movement of the British army.

Rebecca was hopeful she would have a chance to see Oliver and her father at this camp. It had been five days since they left Valley Forge, and she was anxious to see them before the armies came to their inevitable conflict. She spent the day involved in chores and helping other camp followers and soldiers situated nearby. She made up her mind that after dinner, if she had not heard from Oliver or her father, she would seek them out. It was immediately after dinner in the early evening that Hut showed up at her tent.

"Miss Rebecca, I want you to come wit me," is all Hut said.

Gabriel sat, exhausted from the day's activities. Each day he felt more tired than the day before. No matter how much rest he got, he could not recover from the physical demands of each day. They had already lost several men to heat stroke and would probably lose more before they even went to battle. He wondered how Rebecca was faring in the heat and chastised himself for not checking in on her. But the truth was he needed total rest every day and lacked the energy to wander about in search of her. He determined that after dinner, when the temperatures cooled a bit, he would pay her a visit.

The army and its followers were sprawled all over the Hart farm, and Gabriel made his way through the planted fields, looking for Rebecca, but there was no sign of her. Finally he spotted Mehti's friend, Isaiah, and his mother sitting outside their tent in the corn field, and he approached them.

"Excuse me," Gabriel said as he removed his hat. "Have you seen my daughter, Rebecca?"

"Yes, of course, she is sharing our tent with us. But she isn't here right now."

"Is she doing all right? Do you know where she is?"

"She is fine. Such a strong young woman. She left here maybe an hour ago with the Negro soldier, Hut. They were headed in that direction," the woman said as she pointed across the field toward a wooded area.

Gabriel tried not to show the sense of alarm that spread through his body. He didn't want to overreact, but something was amiss.

Stuttering a bit he said, "Thank you, madam. I will continue my search for her," and he backed away. Gabriel spent the next hour and a half wandering through the fields of the farm, looking for his daughter and Hut. He walked to the edge of the woods, calling her name, but with no response. He wondered if he should go find Oliver and set out in search of her in the wooded areas around the farm. Of course, it was possible she and Hut were simply running errands around the campsite. But there had been no sign of them. As darkness took hold, Gabriel decided to go back to her tent to see if she had returned. If she had not, he determined he would wait there for her. Surely she would return before long.

When he circled back to Rebecca's tent, there was still no sign of her. Beside himself with worry, Gabriel settled down among the cornstalks, with five yards and a clear line of vision between him and the tent entrance, and waited. It did not take long before Rebecca and Hut appeared, making their way through the corn. Gabriel saw them pause at the tent entrance. Hut took her hand and patted it saying, "It gonna be all right, Miss Becca."

As Hut turned to leave, Gabriel rose up and flew at Hut in a rage, shoving him and knocking him to the ground.

"What goes on here?" he yelled at Hut as he pinned him to the ground, his face full of fury within inches of Hut's.

Rebecca was startled by her father's assault. She tried to pull him off Hut. "Father, what are you doing? You must remove yourself. Hut has done nothing wrong."

Gabriel raised his fist, about to strike Hut, when Rebecca grabbed his arm in an attempt to stop him. A thwarted blow grazed the side of Hut's face.

"I's just doin' as I is told," Hut yelled up at Gabriel. "Please, Massa White, I just doin' as I's told," Hut repeated.

"Told by whom? And what have you done?" Gabriel demanded.

"Captain Tewkesbury. He ask me to fetch her. Cus of the war comin'. So I fetch her so they can be together cus of the war comin'," Hut answered, his voice high pitched and rapid, hoping to avoid another blow to his face that, if delivered, would most likely hit its mark.

Gabriel looked up at his daughter. "Is this true, Rebecca? Did you leave the camp to be with Oliver?"

Rebecca began to sob as Gabriel got up off Hut and offered him a hand to pull him to his feet.

"I see," Gabriel said.

"I had to go to him," Rebecca pleaded. "He could be killed in the days to come. I had to be with him just this one time. I have been so fretful for you all these last few days, I jumped at the chance to be with Oliver. Hut took me to a rendezvous point in a wooded area and left us so we could be together," she sobbed through her words. "Father, he asked me to marry him," she added. "He intended to speak with you first, but now your presence here has pressed the issue."

Gabriel in stood silent disbelief momentarily, glaring down at his daughter. Then his face calmed.

"Can you understand why a man would want to seal a vow before going into battle?" Rebecca asked him.

"Of course I can. And I can see no reason why he would not make a good husband for you, although I know not his family or his financial circumstances. That all seems rather inconsequential at this moment."

"Oliver was going to speak with Captain McLane, or perhaps General Wayne could marry us. We hoped to marry tomorrow."

His demeanor now changed, Gabriel hugged his daughter and kissed her on the forehead. "I will go and find Oliver and let him know that I give you both my blessing."

Chapter 31

On June 24, 1778, Oliver's fellow officer, Captain Allan McLane, officiated at an exchange of vows between Oliver Tewkesbury and Rebecca White in a grove not far from the farmhouse of John Hart. The only other people in attendance were Gabriel and Hut. The ceremony was brief, no more than five minutes, but no less official.

In preparation, Rebecca washed her one dress and had Isaiah's mother hang it out to dry in a nearby tree. She also washed her hair with soap, for the first time in a few weeks, in a bucket of water and combed out the tangles. Oliver looked splendid and commanding in his uniform.

"This is not the wedding I would have wanted for us," Oliver told Rebecca before the ceremony started as he held her hands in his, the gaze of his soft grey eyes sealed to hers. He brought her hands to his lips and gently kissed them. "I would have wanted our families here. But I want you for my wife forever and, in spite of the circumstances in which we find ourselves, in my heart I am full of joy that you will be my wife."

Rebecca's mind conjured up the first time she had met Oliver, a stranger who had careened through her front door in Granville two years earlier, delirious with smallpox fever. How far they had come in so many ways. Now this handsome, brave and loving man would be her husband. She didn't care about the circumstances. She was just so happy to be his bride.

A canopy of boughs hung over their heads like the ceiling of a chapel and provided welcome shade—a sanctuary from the heat, even at the early hour. Gabriel stood at Rebecca's side, his head bowed, his hands clasped in front of him. He too felt the joy of the occasion. Hut had never been to such a ceremony and was happy to see his two friends get married.

"Oliver, please repeat after me," Captain McLane began. And in less than five minutes, "I now pronounce you husband and wife." Then he swiftly shook Oliver's hand, "Congratulations, Captain, but please excuse me," and he swiftly exited to return to more-pressing responsibilities.

Oliver kissed Rebecca and hugged her, then received congratulatory handshakes from Gabriel and Hut.

"We must return to our men," Oliver told Rebecca. After another hug and a kiss on her forehead, and a hug and kiss from her father, the three men left Rebecca and headed toward the encampment. Even though they were now husband and wife, as per Washington's directives, camp followers, even wives, were not permitted to tent with their spouses. Rebecca had no idea when she would see Oliver again.

The next day was uneventful, and on the morning of June 26, the army broke camp and headed for Kingston some ten miles away and perhaps within twenty miles of the British Army.

Chapter 32

The town of Kingston turned out to be a brief respite of a one-night stay when word reached the main army that General Lee and his advance troops were positioned just outside of Englishtown, near where the English were camped at Monmouth Courthouse. Washington determined to immediately move the main body of the army forward early the next morning, headed also for Englishtown, a one-day's march.

Rebecca was so relieved to see Oliver walking toward her tent as thunderous clouds billowed overhead and rumbles could be heard approaching from a distance. The sky was darkening forebodingly, casting an ominous pall over the campsite, electrifying the air with a sense of urgency. Oliver took Rebecca in his arms and kissed her.

"Not the best way to start a marriage," Oliver said, kissing her again on the forehead and brushing aside a long strand of her blonde wispy hair.

"You mustn't worry about such things right now, Oliver. You've more important things to consider. We will have our time once this war is done with," Rebecca said smiling up at him.

"It looks like we're in for a downpour," Oliver said, looking skyward. "Good thing your tent has been pitched. We may be moving on to Monmouth Court in the morning to engage the British. Our scouts tell us they've paused at that site a few miles from Englishtown. We've been instructed to leave all our belongings, packs and bedding in Englishtown when we march. But I come with a word of instruction for you, Rebecca, because I don't know if I'll get to see you again until after the battle. Once the camp followers get to Englishtown, please, stay with the baggage. Do not follow the troops or venture onto the field of battle. I know you and appreciate your desire to help the injured, but I wouldn't want anything to happen to you, my dearest. A detail will collect the wounded and bring them back to Englishtown for medical attention. I want you to promise me you'll stay in Englishtown."

"I promise. I can stay to the rear. But surely the men will need my assistance, especially if all the men become engaged and there's no one to gather the fallen. There could be wounded and those overcome with the heat. I should be there to help them. I will be cautious, I promise you. And what about you, Father and Hut? You must be careful as well. Anything can happen on a battlefield. But you can guard your lives to some extent, can you not?" Rebecca paused, collecting her thoughts. "It's good to be brave, but not foolhardy is all I'm saying."

"We leave in the morning, and I will return to Englishtown and to you as soon I can. Hut will be marching with me and, I suppose, the militia and your father as well. I will pass your words of caution on to them." Oliver gave her one parting kiss and then fled back toward his regiment. Within five minutes, the skies opened and a torrential rain that lasted all night soaked the encampment.

In the morning, the march began at first light. Crystal-clear blue skies allowed the sun to beat down on a cumbersome trail muddied from the night's rain. The horses and wagons labored to move forward with as much haste as conditions would permit. Again, the heat continued to rise up over 90 degrees and the humidity lingered, making the journey more harrowing. After having traveled several days, Rebecca felt emotionally and physically weakened. She thought of the hardship the men would be facing in the next few days and, with each muddied foot lifted, she determined to strengthen her resolve for their sake. It was well past midday when they arrived at Englishtown. The main army of six thousand men and their followers had covered a distance of seventeen miles, one of their toughest days.

Rebecca was so relieved to finally sit down that, within a few minutes, she simply collapsed and lay in the grass, along with many others. General Washington had positioned his headquarters in the Englishtown Inn in the center of town. The men began to set up camp, uncertain when they would be called upon to join up with Lee's forces that had been ordered to engage the British. But Rebecca heard no sounds of battle, no cannon blasts or muskets being fired.

Early the next morning, word came that the British Army was beginning its march toward the ocean. The men were ordered to form their columns and began their two-mile march toward Monmouth Courthouse. Rebecca stood on the side of the road, her eyes scanning the passing men, earnestly looking for signs of Oliver, her father or Hut as columns marched by to the cadence of drums and fife. She looked for Oliver's regimental flag to narrow her visual search, but did not see it. Even among the militia that took up the rear of the columns, she could not identify or make eye contact with her father—eye contact that seemed so important at this moment. The men of her life were three among thousands, on their way to battle.

The followers were asked to prepare for incoming wounded, using whatever means they had at their disposal for bedding, bandages, water and medicines. Rebecca, Isaiah and his mother searched for and gathered as many containers as they could find to fill with water from local wells and a nearby stream. Then they waited.

Chapter 33

Hut had difficulty hearing the commands from the front of his column as they began the two-mile march to Monmouth Courthouse. General Washington and his key officers led the procession on horseback. In spite of his inability to hear well, the penetrating beat of the drums helped Hut keep in step. Oliver was marching just three rows in front of him. As far as he knew, Gabriel was far at the rear of the column with the rest of the New England militia. Behind the militia, men and horses pulled several cannons, followed by wagons loaded with ammunition. Since word was the British were already underway, also headed east, the army would likely have to march beyond Monmouth Courthouse to encounter the enemy.

The troops were high spirited, although their energy was depleted from previous days' travels, and temperatures were again soaring on this day. They had only covered a mile or so when Hut noticed two men tending to a soldier who had fallen out of line and staggered to the ground, already overcome by heat. Hut glanced over at the soldier as they passed him, lying flat on his back on the weedy side of the road. His comrades were pouring water on his face, trying to revive him. *Must be from way up north,* Hut thought of the soldier as they marched on by.

Before they even reached Monmouth Courthouse, a buzz of inquiry made its way through the troops, and they halted momentarily. Running up the road from the opposite direction were a large number of continentals in a hasty retreat. Men from Lee's advance army were heading straight for Washington and the main army. The men around Hut all looked at one another, trying to figure out what was happening. Hut could just make out Washington's figure in the distance, and it appeared he motioned to the retreating men to head to the back of the column. Hut watched at least a hundred men run past him.

At one point the soldier next to him asked, "What's happening?" to a passing soldier headed in the opposite direction.

The man just shrugged. "Lee just told us to retreat, so we did," the soldier replied. None of the passing men was injured or even looked fatigued. They certainly did not appear to have faced a battle.

A commotion seemed to be taking place at the head of the column, and it began to move in earnest as Washington put his horse to a trot. The men were forced to pick up their pace. Hut slipped his musket from his shoulder and held it across his chest as he began jogging alongside his fellow soldiers.

As soon as they reached farmland on the other side of Monmouth Courthouse, the road sloped down and Hut caught a panoramic view of what would be the battlefield. He could hear the blasts of muskets coming from across two ravines, beyond which stood the British rear guard. Washington was taking fire as he galloped across the front, shouting instructions to his officers. Many of Lee's men were still retreating across a narrows between the two ravines. The first brigades of the main army were ordered to position themselves to protect the retreating men, but many were felled before making it to safety.

So this is war, Hut thought as he felt an adrenaline rush that gave the illusion of invincibility.

"Hut, stay with me," Oliver commanded as he and the entire brigade followed orders to station themselves at the army's left flank. The men careened across a field and crouched below some brush at the top of an embankment overlooking the west ravine. With the British easily discernible on the opposite side, they opened fire.

"You's a better shot den me," Hut said to Oliver. "I load, you shoot." The two men swapped muskets while Hut stayed crouched behind, repeatedly reloading Oliver's musket. Then came the deafening cannon blasts from the British, one striking not twenty feet away. Two men situated near them took the shot straight on and were sent airborne, their body parts landing several feet from their original position, the cannon ball spewing dirt in every direction.

Hut could see off to his right, toward the center of the battle, men struggling to push several cannons into place in answer to the British bombardment, and noticed that Gabriel was one of those assisting in that effort. For the next two hours, both armies were consumed by a grueling artillery duel that caused numerous casualties on both sides, and provided no advancement for either. A tug of panic grabbed Hut when he realized they were becoming low on ammunition. The two men were sweating so profusely, it was impossible to keep the salty substance from stinging their eyes and clouding their vision.

"We need more gunpowder," Hut yelled at Oliver over the roar of cannons.

"There are stores behind the lines. I'll go refill our power horns," Oliver screamed at Hut. He turned and ran to the back of the line toward a weathered barn at the edge of the field, where he believed extra munitions were being stored.

Hut crouched down and scurried across the front toward the cannons, intending to relieve Gabriel who had, for the previous two hours, been loading balls. He wove his way past several wounded men who cried out, and many who did not. Hut stopped to assist an injured soldier seated in the field, his face contorted in pain as he held his motionless left arm close to his side. Hut gave him a comforting pat on the shoulder and pointed to a medical detail with a stretcher headed in his direction.

A dolly of cannon balls was being pushed by three men toward the cannon Gabriel was servicing, to replenish its shot. Hut leaned his shoulder into the dolly to help push it through the loose, sandy soil. One of the men said something to him, but the noise from artillery fire was so loud, Hut couldn't make out what he was saying.

When the dolly was in place just behind the cannon, Hut was about to tap Gabriel on the shoulder to relieve him when he looked skyward and saw an airborne cannonball headed directly for them. Without hesitation, he leapt at Gabriel and the two of them tumbled, then,

209

conjoined, rolled away from the cannon ball's impact. Where just one second before there were the three men Hut assisted, plus a gunner and two artillery officers, there now was nothing but their cannon, laid to waste on its side.

Hut lay atop Gabriel, a painful ringing in his ears—then silence.

Oliver ran back to the holding area about a tenth of a mile behind the front. He was astonished at the bravery he had witnessed during the battle. Washington had spent most of the day on the battlefield atop his horse, encouraging his men, directing troop movement—a shining example of bravery.

Just outside the barn, several men were refilling their canteens and splashing water on themselves from a horse trough. Oliver did likewise, then made his way inside to load up on gunpowder. The inside of the barn was stifling, its loft doors closed, prohibiting even the slightest cross breeze. The smell of oats and dung filled the air, as did the agonizing cries of the wounded, since it also served as a holding location for the injured until someone became available to evacuate them to Englishtown. Hearing their cries, Oliver's disdain for the British grew to a fevered pitch, and he was more determined than ever to return to the fight as quickly as possible.

Exiting the barn at the rear, he rounded the building, headed back to the battlefield, when he noticed a soldier sitting upright against the barn. He appeared to be sleeping, his musket lying across his lap. Incensed,

Oliver strode up to him to admonish his cowardice. Oliver shook him awake, but the man simply fell over, another victim of heat stroke, Oliver surmised.

"Blasted!" Oliver yelled out in frustration. Then he grabbed the soldier's musket and ran toward the battlefield and back to the position he and Hut had held, but he saw no sign of Hut. Bullets flew past him as the British increased their musketry assault. Within ten yards of his former battle station, Oliver was careened back by a bullet and stumbled, falling into the tall grass. Lying there, he looked skyward and noted the beauty of the drifting clouds, something he hadn't noticed all day. He knew he had been hit, but didn't feel any significant pain—just a slight tingling to the left of his abdomen. He reached down with his left hand and felt the wetness. Bringing his blood-soaked hand before his eyes confirmed he had taken shot. Thinking of Rebecca, Oliver put his hand over his heart. *Rebecca will be so upset with me for getting wounded,* he thought.

Rebecca spent most of the day assisting the medics and doctors caring for the wounded. The thunderous sound of the war was frightening, even from two miles away. She couldn't imagine what it must be like for the soldiers. The doctors had performed several amputations to save the lives of those seriously wounded. Rebecca simply piled the limbs outside the makeshift hospital tent, certain that someone would take responsibility to bury them after the battle. What she knew now was that she was exhausted, but dared not give into her exhaustion as

211

she watched two doctors work unceasingly to do whatever they could to save lives.

Toward the late afternoon, the sound of cannon and gun fire came to a halt. Rebecca remembered her promise to Oliver not to venture onto the battlefield. She exited the tent and witnessed men returning from Monmouth Courthouse—worn out, broken men. She looked for Oliver, Hut and her father, but saw no sign of them. *I can stand this no longer.* Grabbing a canteen, Rebecca headed down the road toward Monmouth Courthouse and the battlefield beyond. Within half a mile, she saw Hut assisting her father along the roadway, her father's arm draped limply over Hut's broad shoulders. She waved and called to them, but they did not respond. Rebecca ran up to them while she searched the retreating men for a sign of Oliver.

"Are you injured?" Rebecca asked her father, instinctively feeling his torso. He pointed to his ears and shook his head, no. Searching Hut's eyes, she asked, "What has happened?" Hut also pointed to his ears and shook his head. "Where is Oliver?" she asked frantically. They both continued to shake their heads and point to their ears. As far as Rebecca could tell, they had both lost their hearing.

"I need to go find Oliver," she said, realizing as she ran down the road that she was only talking to herself.

Chapter 34

Mehti opened her eyes and let out a soft whimper as she looked into the relieved eyes of Ruby Tumms.

"Well, hello there, Miss Mehti. You been mighty sick, chile."

Mehti closed her eyes again.

"Das right, girl, you get all the sleep you need. Your fever broke yesterday, so you on the mend, fo' shore. But you sleep now. The body knows what it needs. Ruby be here when you ready to get up and around."

Ruby had stayed at Mehti's side day and night, tending to her every need. Just seeing the girl open her eyes filled Ruby with a calming relief. It had been ten days since the army had evacuated Valley Forge, and few soldiers or camp followers remained behind. Ruby had no idea when Rebecca and Gabriel would return for Mehti. And she worried for her friend, Hut. But there was plenty of wood, food and water remaining at Valley Forge, enough to last them up to a month, she reckoned. Those remaining behind had received no word about the whereabouts or condition of the army. Once it left, Valley Forge became a ghost of its past, a place of hardship and rebuilding, never to be visited again.

Over the previous few days, Mehti had become well enough for Ruby to wander the camp investigating the vacated cabins in search of anything left behind that might add to their comfort. But precious little had been left behind. In the long house she found some swatches of rawhide and some sinew; she decided to make herself some moccasins that would make her next hike more bearable. Once she finished her own, she started on a second pair for Mehti, whose feet had been somewhat affected by a loss of skin from the pox.

Mehti's smallpox had been one of the mildest cases Ruby had ever seen, but still the girl suffered with high fevers, delusions and a moderate rash. Ruby expected she would suffer no scaring, which was a blessing for so young a child.

As Ruby sat outside Mehti's tent, working on her moccasins, she considered her options once Rebecca and Gabriel returned for their daughter. Her former master had set her free when he decided to explore the west. But freedom for Ruby meant starvation as she had no means of supporting herself. The day he set her free, she was mixed with the emotions of both joy and worry. Out of necessity, she decided to become a camp follower because the men paid her for cooking, washing and mending.

Then she met Hut Tewkesbury—a good man, a kind man. The kind of man a woman could make a life with, she thought. During war, life was so uncertain, she dared not think much of the future. One thing she did know for now was that wherever the army ended up was most likely where she would have to travel to next.

Her thoughts were interrupted by a pat on her shoulder. She turned and looked up at Mehti standing over her. "Oh my, Mehti girl. What you doing? You should not be up, chile." Ruby put down her sewing and Mehti slid into her lap and felt the safe, caring warmth of Ruby's enfolding arms.

Chapter 35

The previous chaos of the battlefield settled down by an unspoken mutual understanding. The men on both sides of the conflict were exhausted from the fight, and a pause was welcome by both armies.

Rebecca reached the edge of the field and scanned the broad expanse divided by the two ravines that separated the British from the American army. Nearby she could see Continental soldiers busy retrieving the wounded and dead, loading them on wagons headed for Englishtown. Looking across the eastern and western ravines to the British position, she could see their men engaged in the same activity.

While all was presently quiet, it was possible the battle would resurface at any time, and Rebecca was aware there were risks in her being there. Undaunted, she ran directly to the army's front, where soldiers still able were told to remain and hold their ground in case fighting resumed. In truth, they were all hoping to hold off any more confrontation until the next day.

Rebecca made her way up to the front line and approached several groups of soldiers sitting or lying on the ground, waiting and watching for any activity. "Do you know Oliver Tewkesbury? Have you seen him?" she asked soldiers at each position she visited. The men all just shook their heads. Panic and despair swirled within her. Perhaps Oliver had made it back to Englishtown and she bypassed him among retreating troops. She spun around in circles, looking in every direction, straining to see where he might be. There were several details out in the field, teams of two men, and several wagons used for carting off those who needed medical attention, and those who were to be buried.

Glancing up toward the field between her and a barn, about fifty yards away, two men were placing a soldier on a stretcher. She just knew it was Oliver. "Oh, thank God," she cried out, and started running in their direction. When she got within ten feet of the stretcher, she was taken aback by the color of his pallid skin—flesh void of blood—and she knew Oliver was gone. She now moved slowly to his side, "Oh, Oliver," she gasped. The two men put the stretcher back down on the ground.

"Is this your husband, ma'am?" one of the soldiers asked. Rebecca looked at him blankly, then slowly nodded her head. "We'll leave you to your grieving, ma'am," the other soldier said tipping his hat. The two men moved on to perform their grisly task elsewhere in the field.

Rebecca knelt by Oliver's body and began to weep. His face was so calm and his wounds so unapparent, one might think he were just napping. But there was no breath, no pulse and no sign of life. In the heat of the day, his body had already stiffened in death. She lay across his body, hugging him, wishing him to lift up his arms to hold her one more time. *How could this have happened?* Rebecca knew there were risks involved with war, but it honestly never occurred to her that Oliver would do anything but return to her. It never crossed her mind for an instant. Like her brother, Jacob, she figured Oliver might lose a limb, or need to have a bullet removed from his leg. But never did it occur to her that he would be killed. Now she sobbed unrelentingly until the two soldiers returned to retrieve Oliver's body.

"Ma'am, you best come with us in the wagon back to Englishtown. You can help pick out where you'd like your husband buried, if you like. But we need to clear him away."

"Yes, of course," Rebecca stammered, realizing she was in shock.

The ride back to Englishtown was a blur. Rebecca kept turning around to view Oliver's jostling body lying among others in the bed of the wagon. She felt numb. What would she do now? She needed to talk with her father, but he could not even hear her words. It felt like life was being drawn out of her as well.

When they reached Englishtown, a section of ground had been set aside for burials, and the two men proceeded to unload their wagon. Rebecca felt unable to move. When all the bodies had been removed, it was clear the men needed to return to the battlefield to retrieve more.

Rebecca stepped down from the wagon and sat on the ground by Oliver's body, her eyes locked on his face—a face she would never see again. *How can this be?* she thought over and over. A slight cooling breeze swept across her face that was mildly comforting in some way. She watched as several men began to dig Oliver's grave. *I have so little time left to see his face.* It was all happening so fast. She reached out and gently touched the golden-brown highlights in his hair. She suddenly realized she would never look into his loving, grey eyes again. She was sure her heart would stop beating.

Rebecca was vaguely aware that someone was standing beside her; she looked up to see her father staring down at her. He too had been gazing down at the body of Oliver Tewkesbury in disbelief. He reached for her and lifted her up, enveloping her in his arms.

"I'm so sorry, Becca."

"Can you hear me, Father? What am I to do now?" But Gabriel shook his head, pointing to his ears. "I cannot hear you, Rebecca." Rebecca nodded in acknowledgement.

"Come with me," he said. "Don't stay here and watch this."

But Rebecca pulled away from him, refusing to leave Oliver's side. She watched as they lowered his unwrapped body into the hole and began to cover him with loose dirt. It was only when his body was totally covered, and she could see him no more, that Rebecca turned away and walked back to the campsite, her father holding on to her tightly.

"Tomorrow we fight another day," he said to her. "It looks like both Hut and I have lost our hearing. It could be temporary or permanent—we just don't know at this point. I don't know how good soldiers we'll make if we can't hear orders. But I'm ready to fight. I can still man a cannon."

Rebecca just looked at him, knowing it was pointless to respond. He delivered her back to her tent, kissed her on the cheek and returned to his unit.

The next morning, when the troops rose to begin the second day of battle, the British army was nowhere to be seen. In the middle of the night the British silently evacuated and spent the night marching toward Sandy Hook to board ships headed for New York. Word was spread that General Washington opted not to pursue.

Chapter 36

Hut, Rebecca and Gabriel sat by the side of the road, watching the Continental Army march past—heading north for New Brunswick some sixteen miles distant, then on to White Plains, New York. It had been four days since the British evacuated the battlefield. The planned stop in New Brunswick would give the men an opportunity to rest and bathe in the Raritan River. They anticipated arriving on July 4th, the second anniversary of the signing of the Declaration of Independence. The men were hopeful that a ration of rum would be part of the celebration.

The stop in New Brunswick would also provide an opportunity to begin the first steps in a court-martial of General Charles Lee, accused by Washington of disobedience of orders for not attacking the enemy at Monmouth Courthouse on the 28th, for misbehavior before the enemy for directing a disorderly, cowardly retreat, and for disrespect of the commander-in-chief.

As the soldiers passed by, every time an opening occurred between the units, Hut showed his frustration by picking up a small rock and tossing it across the road. He hadn't heard what Captain McLane had said to him and Gabriel two days before, but he understood the message. The Captain shook their hands and thanked them for their service. Hut was honorably discharged due to the loss of his hearing. As a minuteman, and not officially a member of the Continental Army, Gabriel, who also suffered total hearing loss, was free to stay or go as he chose. He was choosing to leave. Then the Captain turned to Rebecca.

"My deepest condolences, Mrs. Tewkesbury," Captain McLane said, taking Rebecca's hand in his. "So short a marriage—Oliver's loss is quite hard to absorb. I'm sure you must be devastated. But these are the costs of war. I leave you with his personal effects," he said as he handed over Oliver's satchel, canteen and bedroll. Oliver's musket had been scavenged from the field and loaded on a weapons wagon headed north also. "And please let your father and Private Hut Tewkesbury know that, should they ever regain their hearing and want to return to the fight for freedom, they will be more than welcome."

It took less than an hour for the entire army to pass by, including the contingency of Oneidas, numerous supply wagons, towed cannons and camp followers. Rebecca had said goodbye to her fellow camp mates and wished them Godspeed, knowing she would likely never see them again.

They watched as the army disappeared down the road, then all was eerily quiet, like the calm after a storm. Across from the burial ground, nearly three hundred men had been buried, at least one hundred of whom had succumbed to heat stroke. A makeshift hospital had been set up to tend the wounded who would also stay behind until they were well enough to travel. Many were amputees who would be sent home. Others would become well enough to rejoin the army at some point.

"We need to hike to Valley Forge," Gabriel said to Rebecca. "We need to collect Mehti and figure out how we're going to get back to Connecticut."

Mehti—with the raging of the battle and the loss of Oliver, Rebecca had given Mehti not one thought. All of a sudden, she felt a panicking urgency to get to Valley Forge as soon as possible. *Mehti must be well—she simply must. I cannot bear another loss,* she thought. Turning to her father, she held up her index finger, a sign she needed a minute. She walked across the road toward the burial ground to say a final goodbye to Oliver. The burial locations had each been marked by small wooden posts, but they were not designated. Oliver's gravesite was now one of many, and Rebecca could not remember exactly which plot was Oliver's. She stood looking up and down the rows. As on the day Oliver died, a soft breeze had gently caressed her cheek, and she felt grateful for this soothing comfort of nature.

"Goodbye, Oliver," Rebecca whispered quietly, standing on the edge of the burial plot, not knowing where to direct her sight. One of these graves held Oliver. That's all she knew.

"Come along, Rebecca, we need to leave," Gabriel said gently as he stepped up behind her and took her by the elbow, prompting her away. She nodded and looked toward Hut. Her father read her mind, and signaled to Hut that they were leaving, and that Hut was welcome to come with them. Hut nodded, a look of gratitude on his face, and the three began their trek back to Valley Forge, seventy miles away.

The trio took five days to reach Valley Forge. While the weather continued to be brutally hot, the rain held off for their entire trip. Gabriel and Hut foraged for berries and mushrooms, and hunted for rabbit and squirrel. Rebecca hauled water and cooked whatever they brought back to their campsites, which were generally located off the main road to avoid unscrupulous highwaymen. It was comforting to know they need not fear British harassment.

The entire trip was enshrouded in an absence of conversation. Occasionally Rebecca would communicate with her father by writing messages in the dirt with a stick. And he would reply verbally. Hut's reading skill was limited, so her communication with him consisted mostly of sign language. At one point when Gabriel was watching Rebecca use hand signs to communicate with Hut, he turned to her and said, "We must teach Hut to read," which brought a smile to Rebecca's face and warranted a hug for her father.

On their last day before arriving back at Valley Forge, the three stopped to rest and have a drink of water beneath the welcoming shade of a huge maple tree. A flock of agitated grackles was perched overhead, screeching some kind of loud discontent—a deafening cackle. But it was not deafening for Hut, who suddenly stopped drinking and lowered his canteen. A broad smile came across his face, and he pointed to his ears. "I hear something!" he said with glee. "I hear something!"

Rebecca quickly moved toward him and crouched down, looking directly into his face, shouting, "Can you hear me, Hut?" Hut nodded slowly, then held his thumb and forefinger an inch or so apart, indicating "a little."

Rebecca's face lit up with joy. "That's a start, Hut. That's something. The doctor said your loss might be temporary. It looks like he may be right," she shouted at him. He nodded in response, a smile so broad it could have spanned the Delaware.

Crossing the Schuylkill River Bridge and entering Valley Forge felt like returning to a deserted home. Isaac Potts, whose stone house had been used as Washington's headquarters during the occupation, had returned and could be seen tending the kitchen garden. He must have recognized the trio, because he waved to them from across the grounds. They waved back. The broad, empty expanse of their former encampment held such harsh memories, especially for Rebecca, who had nursed so many of the sick, and held the hands of the dying. In spite of those memories that washed over her as they entered Valley Forge, Rebecca felt grateful for what was a bit of a homecoming.

The three of them immediately headed for Mehti's tent, uncertain what they would find. Of course, they had received no word of her condition while traveling with the army, so her situation was unknown to them. They walked behind the cabins of the enlisted men where once had stood more than three hundred tents used by camp followers—and where now there stood one lone tent. Rebecca picked up her stride, her heart pounding, her mind reeling as she tried to prepare herself for what they might find. Aside from Isaac Potts, there was not another

soul in sight. It was the end of a long, hot, arduous day—
one where they had covered the most miles of any other
day, so eager to get to Valley Forge. Rebecca wasn't sure
of the date, but she thought it to be around July 6th or 7th.

When they reached Mehti's tent, they dropped
their packs and Rebecca flung open the flap to find the
tent empty, with no sign of activity. There was no fire in
the pit or even dying embers to evidence a cooked
morning meal. Rebecca felt that same panic in her chest
she had when Mehti went missing at the wharf in
Philadelphia. The three of them returned to the
encampment's grand parade, scanning in all directions in
search of Mehti and her caregiver, Ruby.

It was then they spotted two figures in the
distance, one tall carrying a bucket, and one short, both
moving slowly across the field of new sprouting grass
that had in the recent past witnessed the trampling of
thousands of marching, drilling soldiers. Rebecca ran in
their direction with Hut and Gabriel following. In spite of
her resolve to remain strong and not break down, she felt
tears of joy streaming down her cheeks. When she
reached Mehti, she dropped to her knees and hugged her
sister.

"Thank God you are all right," she said as she
brushed Mehti's hair away from her sallow face so she
could get a good look at her.

"She doing fine, Miss Becca," Ruby said. "Jus' a
little weak, is all."

Mehti's arms were thin like chicken legs. Her
cheeks were sunken and dark circles encased her eyes.

But her smile was bright and that was all Rebecca could hope for. Her father lifted her up and she wrapped her arms around his neck.

"Thank you so much, Ruby," Rebecca said.

"You done good, Ruby," Hut added as he smiled at her, rubbed her back and gave her a quick peck on the cheek. Rebecca was a bit surprised to see their affection. She had no idea Ruby was anything other than an acquaintance of Hut's. But it was clear the two had made a connection.

Mehti lifted her head from her father's shoulder and looked around. "Where's Oliver?"

Rebecca's heart lost the joy of the moment, her shaky voice responding, "He didn't make it, Mehti. They buried him by the battlefield where he was shot and killed," she said just above a whisper. Rebecca wondered what she could possibly do to console her sister when she found her own grief so consuming. But Mehti showed amazing strength, or perhaps she was physically too weak to show any grief.

"Was he a hero?" she asked.

"He fought bravely," Rebecca replied.

A faint smile emerged on Mehti's lips. "I will never forget him.

"Me neither, Mehti. Me neither."

Chapter 37

The July weather continued to swelter. Rebecca kept Mehti out of their tent as much as possible and made a straw bed for her under the shade of a nearby tree, sure the fresh air would improve her health. Mehti was getting stronger every day, and Gabriel felt the time was near for them to venture back to Connecticut. His main concern was whether Mehti was physically able to manage the trip.

Hut's hearing seemed to be improving as well. Hut had already suffered hearing loss before the battle, while Gabriel's hearing had been fine. Now, ironically, it was Gabriel's hearing loss that seemed permanent. Not long after their arrival back at Valley Forge, Rebecca's frustration, communicating with her father using sign language and writing in the dirt with sticks, took hold. It occurred to her that Oliver might have paper, pen and ink among his possessions. The satchel of Oliver's belongings remained in the corner of the tent, and she had not been able to bring herself to open it. She would stare at it nightly, trying to conjure up the courage to touch the things he probably touched last before he died.

Finally, in a moment when no one was around, she sat in the middle of their tent and stared intently at the satchel that lay in her lap. She ran her hands over it as if it were the embodiment of his soul. She hugged it to her chest and inhaled its aromas, hoping for a wisp of his scent. But the odors radiating from the bag were of war — dirt, gun oil, stale cheese and mead.

She gently opened the flap and peaked inside, her heart pounding for some unknown reason. First, Rebecca lifted out a piece of linen that she unfolded as if it held a king's ransom of precious gems. Inside she found a ball of soap, a rather dull razor, a comb and a mirror. In one side of the bag was a rock hard, left-over piece of biscuit with one bite removed. Rebecca unconsciously brought it to her lips knowing Oliver's lips had once been there too. She wanted to cry, but took a deep breath and held back her tears. Also inside the satchel she found a fork, knife, tin plate and cup, a tinder box that contained flints, a ball of twine and several fish hooks. *The sum of necessary provisions in an army man's life,* she thought sadly.

At the bottom of the satchel was a pouch with a drawstring. She opened it to find another folded piece of cloth, which she gently unfolded. Inside were four gold coins she surmised were what remained from the monies given to Oliver for their spy mission into Philadelphia.

"Becca?" her father called to her from outside the tent.

She quickly put all Oliver's things back in the satchel, closed the flap and set it aside, holding on to the gold coins, and stepped out of the tent.

"Becca, I feel we need to begin to make plans to return home."

She nodded in agreement.

"Mehti is doing well and while it's a lengthy trip from here to Connecticut, we can take our time, being careful not to tax her too much along the way. We can rest whenever we need to. It's maybe two hundred fifty miles,

I would guess. Jon Bear thought he could make it on his own in fifteen days. Maybe it will take us twenty-five or thirty. It doesn't matter, really. But we need to get started soon." He finally paused after delivering his concerns in rapid succession.

Rebecca held out her hand with the gold coins lying in her palm and smiled up at her father.

Gabriel's eyes opened wide in astonishment. "Where ever did you get that, Becca?" Rebecca reached into the tent and pulled out Oliver's satchel, pointing to it.

"I can't believe it, Becca. With that gold we could book passage from Philadelphia to New London." He was so relieved, he wrapped his arms around her, a show of affection she had rarely seen her father express.

Rebecca picked up a stick and walked over to a clear area of dirt. In the ground she wrote, "Hut?" and looked into her father's eyes.

"I don't know what Hut wants to do with his life."

Rebecca smudged out her first message and wrote, "Is this enough?"

"I think if we bargain, we could gain passage for all of us, but I don't know if Hut would want to come to Connecticut."

Rebecca wrote, "May he?"

"Of course."

Rebecca smiled up at her father and then gave him an unsuspecting hug. "I will go and ask him, Father." Then she turned and ran in the direction of the Schuylkill River, where she knew Hut and Ruby were fishing for their dinner.

"Hut!" Rebecca yelled when she found him, Ruby and Mehti sitting on the river bank, a string of his catch wallowing in the shallows. The three of them turned to her, a bit startled.

Rebecca held out her hand and showed them the coins. "Look what I found at the bottom of Oliver's satchel—four gold coins! I think it's money left over from our trip to Philadelphia. Father believes if we barter properly, it will gain us all passage to Connecticut," she said excitedly. Then she sat down beside them. "Hut, do you want to come to Connecticut?"

"What yo daddy have to say 'bout dat, Miss Becca?"

"He says you are welcome, Hut. We cannot make any guarantees except that we can help you make your way in Granville. My father is well respected and he can help you find work. And you can stay with us until you can find your own place."

Ruby was listening to the conversation and held her vision straight ahead, not knowing what Hut would do. Hut immediately read her concern.

"What about Miss Tumms? She welcome, too?"

"Of course!" Rebecca responded. Even though she hadn't discussed it with her father, she felt certain he would acquiesce and bring them both. After all, Hut had saved her father's life, and Ruby had probably saved Mehti's.

Hut turned to Ruby, "Ruby, what would you say if I asked you to come to Connecticut with me?"

"Are you asking me?" Ruby replied with a sheepish grin on her face. "And what exactly are you asking me, Hut Tewkesbury?"

"You a tough woman, Ruby. I guess I's asking you to have a life wit me. If you willin'?"

"He's a good man, Ruby," Mehti interjected convincingly.

Ruby tucked her arm through Hut's and leaned her head on his shoulder, "I's willin'," Ruby said smiling up at him. Mehti clapped her hands in delight.

"Then it's settled," Rebecca said. "Now all we have to do is decide when to leave. I suspect father would prefer to leave very soon. I'll go speak with him now." And she ran back toward the grand parade and their tent, where her father was preparing a dinner fire. Although it was still oppressively warm, her heart felt buoyed and light by the events of the day.

Chapter 38

Saying goodbye to Valley Forge, for Rebecca, was like saying goodbye to Oliver one more time. She had so many memories, both good and bad, of the last seven months they had spent together—sharing meals, watching soldiers drill, their trip to Philadelphia, tending to the sick, celebrating the French entering the war. As the five travelers exited the vacant compound, they all paused and took one last look at what had been their home for most of the previous seven months. Rebecca reflected that, in spite of the hardship she and Mehti had faced here, she was glad they had come—glad she hadn't sat home uselessly waiting to find out what had happened to Oliver and her father. She was glad they had been able to help.

They carried as much as they could and, due to the fact Mehti was still weak with recovery, both Hut and Gabriel were prepared to carry her, if needed.

"We won't be able to pay for lodging," Gabriel said as they heading down Gulph Road and out of Valley Forge. They all nodded in understanding. He estimated it would take three days' time to walk the eighteen miles to Philadelphia, to give Mehti enough time to rest. Luckily, the weather was dry. Each night they would settle themselves off the roadway, just out of sight of any passersby.

It took exactly three days for them to enter Philadelphia, a partially demolished city showing no semblance of the glory of its recent past. As they entered the city, Rebecca was struck by the devastation that had occurred just since her visit there a few months earlier. Furnishings had been thrown out of windows and lay shattered in the streets. Entire buildings had been demolished or burned, to deny returning patriots their homes. Piles of garbage and excrement were everywhere. Flies and maggots were in a feasting frenzy. Passing by odiferous side streets, they were forced to cover their noses, the smells were so unbearable.

Benedict Arnold's men were assigned to various tasks to help bring the city to order. Some men were guarding the outskirts, while others assisted in cleanup and removal of debris. In front of the statehouse, the British had dug a huge square pit, into which they tossed the carcasses of dead horses and men. As they passed by, Arnold's men were busy hauling dirt to cover the remains. Congress, which had recently returned from York to its former Philadelphia home, would have to meet elsewhere in the city, the stench was so bad.

Approaching the Delaware, they saw crates, barrels and furnishings floating dockside. Some had been tossed into the river by British soldiers, others tossed overboard by ship captains attempting to limit the amount of cargo loyalists brought on board.

Ruby stared about her in wonder and amazement, as she had never seen a city like Philadelphia. Even in its dilapidated state, it was still the largest city in the colonies.

At the end of Market Street, a huge bonfire had been set for burning the piles of scrap wood strewn about the city.

The five travelers walked up and down Front Street in search of a cargo vessel similar to the sloop *Josephine* that had delivered Jon Bear, Rebecca and Mehti to Philadelphia several months before. A cooling breeze off the river provided refreshing relief from inland heat and the stink of the city. The wharf area was a bustle of activity, as usual. Rebecca held Mehti's hand tightly, recollecting the disappearance of her sister amid the crowds during their previous visit. As they passed along Front Street, Rebecca noticed the same fishmonger who had been there in May, hawking his catches. The small terrier that attracted Mehti months before was still there, begging for a morsel. *Some business is as usual*, Rebecca thought.

"This city is a sickbed," Gabriel said to Rebecca. "We need to leave as soon as possible."

Finally, after several passes along many wharfs, they spotted a ship they thought might be suitable, the sloop, *Katy*, which appeared to be about to disembark.

"Rebecca, you will have to negotiate with me," Gabriel instructed as they walked up to the gangplank.

"Is your captain about?" Rebecca asked one of the hands busy carrying goods on board. "We seek passage to New London, Connecticut and were told your ship will pass by there on its way to New Haven."

"I'll get him for you, miss,"

Within a few minutes, the captain was at their side, and they began discussing the option of traveling on the *Katy*. Gabriel offered his thoughts to Rebecca while she bartered as best she could with the captain. In the end, all five of them were granted passage on the ship for all the gold coin they had. Due to lack of space, they would need to sleep on the lower deck; and meals would be limited to one a day, and that would most likely be a porridge of some kind.

"How soon do you leave?" Rebecca asked the captain.

"Within the hour. You'd best get on board now and find your spot for sleeping," the captain told her.

No sooner had they finalized their agreement than they were on board and underway. The seas were relatively calm—as they usually were this time of year, unless a storm were to brew up.

The five travelers huddled below decks, all crowded together in a small space approximately ten by ten feet, Mehti cradled in her sister's lap.

"And when shall you marry?" Rebecca suddenly asked Hut and Ruby. "We could have a wedding in Granville, if you like."

Hut and Ruby just looked at each other, not sure what either had in mind. Finally, Hut said, "Sooner is better," and Ruby nodded.

"Can't the captain marry them?" Mehti chimed in. "I always thought captains could marry people anytime, but especially out at sea."

"I think that's true, Mehti," Rebecca replied. She turned to Hut, "Shall I ask the captain?"

Hut looked at Ruby, who nodded and said, "Oh, yes."

"Do we need some kind of papers?" Hut asked.

"I'm not sure, but I'll find out tomorrow."

The first night at sea was relatively comfortable, despite their being huddled together on their bedrolls, packed like codfish in a barrel. As promised, dinner had been a bowl of porridge for each of them. Afterward, they were so tired from their travels, they were asleep in no time.

In the morning, Rebecca spoke with the captain, who said no paperwork was necessary and he would be happy to perform the marriage ceremony. Then he provided Rebecca with a sheet of paper, ink and a pen and she wrote a message to her father and handed it to him with a smile. It simply said:

Hut and Ruby are to be married tomorrow afternoon.

Gabriel gave her a thumbs up sign and returned the smile.

The next afternoon they were all assembled on the bow of the *Katy*, the captain with his bible in hand, the sun shining down on them like a blessing. The captain's words were brief as they all watched Hut and Ruby gaze lovingly into each other's eyes. When the ceremony was over, the captain handed out tin cups and shared a pint of grog with the four of them that amounted to no more

236

than a sip each. But it set a celebratory tone to the event. Hut turned to the captain, "Do you have a broom?" he asked.

"Why, I'm sure we can find one someplace," he responded, and called on a deck hand to bring a broom. When it appeared, Hut took the broom and laid it on the deck, and together he and Ruby jumped over it.

"There, now it is official," Hut said, and kissed his bride. "We don't have anythin', Ruby, but we gots a new life and dat's a lot," he added.

"Dat's funny, because I feel like I have everything," Ruby said as she hugged Hut.

Ruby and Hut were not provided privacy on their wedding night, but neither seemed to care as long as they were together. Two days after their marriage, the *Katy* sailed easily up the Thames River and docked at a pier off the town of New London.

Chapter 39

Gabriel stepped down from the wagon and spoke to the driver, "Wait here. I'll be right back." He turned toward his home and paused, taking in the welcome sight, then quickly headed for the front door. "Jacob! Jacob! We're home! Quickly, son, bring me a cask of hard cider!" Then he started to laugh, feeling so lighthearted. He was back home and, while his hearing had not returned as he had hoped, he was alive.

Jacob stepped out the door and gasped at the sight of his father, and beyond him, Rebecca and Mehti stepping down from a wagon stopped in front of their house, driven by a man he did not know. "Father!" he shouted, and ran to hug Gabriel. Gabriel lifted him off the ground and spun him around, so happy to see him again. Jacob started to talk to him, but Gabriel pointed to his ears and shook his head.

"Jacob, find Jon Bear and quickly go to the root cellar and bring out a cask of hard cider. This kind man drove us here from New London on the promise of a cask of cider. Please get it straight away."

Jacob hesitated, wanting so much to greet Rebecca and Mehti, but then, thinking better of it, turned and ran to the root cellar behind the house. A few minutes later, as Gabriel and Rebecca were unloading their belongings, Jacob and Jon Bear returned, the cask carried on Jon Bear's shoulder. He brought it to the wagon and loaded it in the back of the bed. Gabriel shook hands with the wagon driver and thanked him for his help getting them to Granville. Tipping his hat, the driver turned his rig around and headed back to New London.

Rebecca and Mehti both hugged Jacob at the same time. "Jacob, it is so good to be home. It is so good to see you," Rebecca exclaimed. Jacob's wife, Rachael came out the front door, her pregnancy now showing, followed by Gabriel's sister, Sarah.

"Oh, my God, we are so grateful you all have returned to us," Sarah said, tears running down her cheeks. She bent down and gave Mehti a hug. Jon Bear shook hands with Gabriel, and patted him on the back in welcome.

For a moment, Rebecca and Mehti stood in silence. "Well, not all of us were able to return," Rebecca said somberly. "Oliver didn't make it. He was shot and killed at a battle in New Jersey," she reported. "And father came close to losing his life in a cannon blast, but he's lost his hearing. We've been hoping it would return, but so far there's been no sign of recovery. But Hut's hearing returned and we are hopeful father's will as well."

Sarah looked at her brother, "Gabriel…" then she realized he could not hear her and went and hugged him.

Hut and Ruby, who had stepped down from the wagon, stood silently by the side of the road, segregated from the reunion, uncertain of their place. Jacob looked over at them, an inquisitive look on his face.

"Oh, my goodness," Rebecca exclaimed when she realized she'd neglected to introduce them. "Jacob, Rachael and Sarah, this is…" she hesitated, then continued. "This is Hut and Ruby Tewkesbury. Hut and

239

Ruby, this is my family—my brother Jacob, his wife Rachael, and my aunt Sarah. And Jon Bear, you know Hut. This is his very new wife, Ruby. They were married at sea on our way here."

"Tewkesbury?" Jacob asked, a confused look on his face.

"It's a long story. I'll explain later. But you should know, Jacob, I am now a Tewkesbury, as well," Rebecca said. "And it's a name I'll hold proudly for the rest of my life. Let's just all go inside and get ourselves settled," she suggested. Then, looking at Hut and Ruby, she added, "We are a newly defined family." She glanced at her father, who must have understood what she said just by reading the expression on her face. He nodded in approval.

They all headed toward the house, Rebecca with her arm around Mehti, Hut with his arm around Ruby. "Father and I will be taking a trip to Brookline to see Oliver's mother and family as soon as we've had some time to rest. We need to let them know he is gone, and of his bravery. I look forward to meeting my mother-in-law."

They walked in quiet reflection for a few moments. "I can't tell you how happy I am to be back home," Rebecca said. Then she said to Mehti, "Tonight you sleep in your own bed."

Tired though she was, Mehti mustered a broad smile.

Epilogue

March 25, 1779

"Push, Miss Becca," Ruby urged as she mopped the perspiration from Rebecca's forehead. "It's time for you to push now. I know we said don't push before, but now it's time."

Rebecca was surrounded by Ruby, Sarah and Rachael, all helping to make her comfortable and assisting Goody Beckham with the birth. Over the decades, midwife Margaret Beckham had delivered more babies than anyone else in Granville. She had not only delivered Rebecca, Jacob and Mehti, but assisted in the births of the four subsequent stillborn babies Rebecca's mother had carried to term.

Goody Beckham sat on a stool at the end of the straw bed, ready to bring Rebecca's child into the world. "The baby is crowning now, Rebecca. You're doing well. I know it's been hours, but I feel sure this baby is ready to birth," she said encouragingly. Rachael and Sarah stood on either side of Rebecca, grasping her hands and lifting her to help push whenever Goody Beckham commanded.

The fall of 1778 and the winter of 1779 were relatively calm times for the Whites and the Tewkesburys. It had taken almost six months for Gabriel to gradually regain his hearing; although it was not as good as it had once been, causing him to often use a listening horn, he was grateful to be able to hear at all and be able to communicate with his family. He cherished his time at

White Horse Tavern on the Granville green, where he would gather news of troop movements, skirmishes and battles. At one point he considered joining the Army again, but the winter of 1779 found Washington and the main army at Morristown, New Jersey reportedly camped under some of the worst winter conditions the army had ever experienced — worse even than Valley Forge. Gabriel fully intended to rejoin the war effort once his second grandchild was born and he knew Rebecca was out of harm's way. Rachael had given birth to a healthy girl on Christmas Day. Again, filled with faith, they named her Anna.

It took only a few weeks after their return from Valley Forge for Hut to find work at a butcher shop in New London, a trade he learned while at the Forge. Gabriel let him ride his mule into town whenever it wasn't needed for plowing, harvesting or clearing land. When the mule wasn't available, Hut would walk the ten miles to work and back each day. Hut, Gabriel and Jon Bear spent their spare time building a lean-to structure on the opposite side of the barn from Jon Bear and Sarah's lodgings. Hut spent his evenings building furniture out of scrap wood, finishing two chairs and a table. Building a fireplace before winter set in was the hardest task, but it was completed just in time for what turned out to be one of the harshest winters ever experienced in New England.

News of Rebecca's pregnancy had shocked Gabriel when she told him. "But how...?" He began to question her, a look of confusion on his face.

Rebecca put her finger to his lips halting his inquiry. "I am sorry if I have disappointed you, Father. I would not hurt you for anything in the world. But you must see that I am so overjoyed to know that Oliver's child grows inside of me. Now he has a legacy, and I will have a piece of him through this child. Please just be happy for me."

Mehti and Sarah were equally happy. The entire family swarmed around Rebecca throughout her entire pregnancy as if she were a queen bee, making sure she didn't work too hard and that she had plenty to eat. Gabriel wrote to Oliver's mother, letting her know she was about to become a grandmother for the first time. Childbirth in Granville was a relatively common occurrence, but this pregnancy, the coming of this child, was viewed by the family as a precious event, especially in light of the losses they had suffered. With the birth of baby Anna, and now Rebecca's baby, the household might be able to overcome the losses they had experienced in recent years—the loss of Anna and Gabriel's stillborn children, the loss of Rachael and Jacob's daughter, and of course, the loss of Oliver, and of Gabriel's wife, Anna. Gabriel in particular hoped the tides of good fortune and providence were finally changing in their favor.

"I am not a greedy man," Gabriel prayed in bed several nights earlier. "I do not want to appear ungrateful for the bounty in my life of family, friends and home. But I ask you, God, to please give us this child, healthy and strong."

"Ughhhh," Rebecca cried out, straining in agony with each contraction.

"You're doing just fine, Rebecca. One or two more good pushes and this baby will be in my arms," Goody Beckham said as she focused her vision on the emerging and ever growing baby's crown. "Sarah, you ready with that string and knife?" she asked. "Any time now—the head is out and the rest should be fairly easy," she said when Rebecca experienced one final contraction and the baby almost jettisoned into Goody Beckham's arms. With the baby lying in her lap, she instantly tied off the umbilical cord and cut it with the knife. She flipped the baby onto its stomach and it instantly began to cry.

Rebecca was so relieved it was over. She looked down at Goody Beckham with a questioning face.

"It's a beautiful boy."

Rebecca began to cry tears of joy, as did Rachael and Sarah. Goody Beckham handed the baby over to Ruby who swabbed him with warm, clean cloths before handing him to his mother, while the midwife tended to the afterbirth.

"Very little bleeding, Rebecca. That's a good thing. You're going to be fine," Goody Beckham said.

Ruby handed the baby to Rebecca who looked down at his beautiful, crying face, and a wave of emotion filled with love swept through her chest. She stroked his head and he calmed and briefly opened his eyes—lovely, soft grey eyes, just like his father's.

"Welcome to this world, Oliver Tewkesbury the second."

The End... for now.

Recommended Reading

Chadwick, Bruce. *The General and Mrs. Washington.* Naperville, Illinois: Sourcebooks, Inc., 2007.

Cott, Nancy F. *The Bonds of Womanhood, Women's Sphere in New England, 1780-1835.* New Haven and London: Yale University Press, 1997.

Fenn, Elizabeth A. *Pox Americana, The Great Smallpox Epidemic of 1775-83.* New York: Hill and Wang, 2001.

Fleming, Thomas. *Washington's Secret War, The Hidden History of Valley Forge.* New York: HarperCollins Publishers, 2005.

Lacey, Barbara E., ed. *The World of Hannah Heaton, The Diary of an Eighteenth- Century New England Farm Woman.* Illinois: Northern Illinois University Press, 2003.

Martin, David Plum. *A Narrative of a Revolutionary War Soldier.* New York: New American Library, 2001.

Norton, Mary Beth. *Liberty's Daughters, The Revolutionary Experience of American Women, 1750-1800.* Ithaca and London: Cornell University Press, 1996.

St. John de Crevecoeur, J. Hector, *Letters from an American Farmer and Sketches of Eighteenth-Century America.* New York: Penguin Classics, 1986.

Washington, George. *The Writings of George Washington from the Original Manuscript Sources, 1745-1799.* Michigan: University of Michigan, 1931.

Connect with me on line:

If you have enjoyed reading my novels, please feel free to provide me with feedback.

E-mail: jogillespie@aol.com
Website: www.jogillespie.com
Facebook: www.facebook.com/JoGillespie

66594235R00153

Made in the USA
Lexington, KY
17 August 2017